The General Councils

The General Councils

A History of the Twenty-One Church Councils from Nicaea to Vatican II

Christopher M. Bellitto

PAULIST PRESS
New York/Mahwah, N.J.

Excerpts from *Decrees of the Ecumenical Councils* edited by Norman P. Tanner are reprinted by permission of Georgetown University Press.

Book design by Theresa M. Sparacio

Cover design by Cheryl Finbow

Cover photo of Vatican Council II courtesy of Catholic News Service, Washington, D.C.

Library of Congress Cataloging-in-Publication Data

Bellitto, Christopher M.
   The general councils : a history of the twenty-one church councils from Nicaea to Vatican II / Christopher M. Bellitto.
      p.   cm.
   Includes bibliographical references and index.
   ISBN 0-8091-4019-5
   1. Councils and synods, Ecumenical. I. Title.
BX825 .B45 2002
262'.52—dc21

                                                      2002005890

Published by Paulist Press
997 Macarthur Boulevard
Mahwah, New Jersey 07430 USA

www.paulistpress.com

Printed and bound in the
United States of America

Contents

v

CONTENTS

For my uncle,
Bishop Robert Brucato,
who shepherds me and the church he serves
closer to the kingdom of God

Acknowledgments

A few years ago, as I was writing *Renewing Christianity: A History of Church Reform from Day One to Vatican II* (Paulist Press, 2001), it became clear that the next logical project should be a history of the church's general councils. This book, therefore, is a sister to *Renewing Christianity;* one can be read without the other, but each would benefit from its sibling.

I am indebted to the many authors of the standard reference works, surveys, histories, and specialized studies on which I relied. My thanks go to the library staffs at St. Joseph's Seminary, Fordham University, and the members of the interlibrary loan system for help with research and materials. I am also grateful to the students and audience members who listened to pieces of these chapters in my courses and public lectures. Their questions and comments often helped me think this material through and pointed out holes that needed to be filled.

I owe some particular debts: to George Pitula, who enthusiastically engaged a number of conciliar and Latin questions; to my doctoral mentor at Fordham University, Louis B. Pascoe, S.J., who encouraged this type of project; to Rev. Francis J. Corry, my first church history teacher, who read the entire manuscript, prompted me to be precise, and made sure I finally focused on a history of the councils; to Kathleen Walsh, who first brought me to Paulist Press for *Renewing Christianity* and signed me on to write this book even before that one was finished; and to Don Brophy, who helped bring the manuscript through its final stages. I will always be thankful for Kathleen and Don's encouragement, positive and nuanced direction, and skillful editing. Finally, I thank Karen Bellitto, my wife and my best friend, for being her and for helping me be me.

Ad maiorem Dei gloriam
C.M.B.

List of General Councils

Councils in the First Millennium
1. Nicaea I — 325
2. Constantinople I — 381
3. Ephesus — 431
4. Chalcedon — 451
5. Constantinople II — 553
6. Constantinople III — 680–681
7. Nicaea II — 787
8. Constantinople IV — 869–870

Councils in the Middle Ages
9. Lateran I — 1123
10. Lateran II — 1139
11. Lateran III — 1179
12. Lateran IV — 1215
13. Lyons I — 1245
14. Lyons II — 1274
15. Vienne — 1311–1312

Councils in the Era of Reformations
16. Constance — 1414–1418
17. Basel-Ferrara-Florence-Rome — 1431–1445
18. Lateran V — 1512–1517
19. Trent — 1545–1548/1551–1552/1562–1563

Councils in the Modern Age
20. Vatican I — 1869–1870
21. Vatican II — 1962–1965

Introduction

Tracing the story of the Catholic Church's twenty-one general councils is one of the best ways to learn about the two-thousand-year course of Christianity. General councils did not consider every aspect of theology and spirituality, but it is almost always true that if something was important, it showed up one way or another at a general council, making these twenty-one major meetings an essential lifeline in church history.

From the start, it may seem odd to talk about councils in church history. They strike us as "democratic" or "constitutional" meetings taking place in a hierarchical church that is presided over by a pope who claims a singular and unique authority directly from Christ. That paradox is one of the most interesting—and sometimes controversial—themes cutting across the history of the twenty-one councils the Roman Catholic Church designates as preeminent.

Another theme is the cycle of challenge-and-response whereby councils met to deal with the problem of heresy, the pressing need for reform, confrontations to the church's authority, and other significant issues pertaining to individual periods of history or cropping up repeatedly throughout Christianity's two millennia. The councils are where the church does her thinking by providing a place and event where problem solving, often at work for decades or even centuries beforehand, can come together in a critical mass. In a general council the church plans how to solve her problems, lays down guiding principles or rules, and organizes the implementation of those plans, principles, and rules. Almost every council follows a pattern: There is a particular motive to call a general council, a period of preparation, the meeting itself, and then the attempt to put its goals into practice.

The fortieth and fiftieth anniversaries of Vatican II's landmark sessions (1962–65) seem the right moment to look back at the prior twenty major councils in church history not only to understand the specific history of each one, but also to put Vatican II and the changes and lively debates it produced into perspective. Publishers produced a batch of books around 1960 to place Vatican II in context after Pope John XXIII made his surprise announcement to call a general council. Because of Vatican II, international scholars have edited and translated the documents of the twenty major councils that preceded it so that we can better understand their history, intentions, and actions. But while there have been many studies of Vatican II and its own very different types of conciliar documents, not enough attention has been paid to the first twenty councils and their documents in light of our own experience of Vatican II.

Even with all of these resources, reading about councils is one thing; living through a council and—armed with that insight—learning about prior councils is quite another. Firsthand familiarity with Vatican II's aftermath gives people today exceptional insight and perspective on how other councils worked. These insights and perspectives make contemporary Christians more fortunate in this regard than the millions of Christians who lived and died during periods when no council met, such as the 306 years between Trent and Vatican I or the ninety two years between Vatican I and Vatican II.

An Overview

This study organizes the twenty-one general councils into the four traditional periods of church history: early, medieval, reformations, and modern. Councils fall into these periods not only because of a certain historical neatness, but because the councils in each of these four eras by and large fit together. Although we will proceed chronologically, we will also be concerned with recurring themes.

Introduction

Broadly speaking, the councils of the first millennium met in order to establish doctrinal statements in the face of heretical alternatives. The medieval and reformation councils dealt with reforming the church and clarifying certain doctrines. The two Vatican councils in the modern period met for very dissimilar reasons: the first to work out a definition of papal infallibility; the second to renew the church, which had for too long lagged behind contemporary developments.

Some councils picked up where the previous one left off; others tried to fix a problem their predecessors failed to solve entirely. The first eight councils, from Nicaea I (325) to Constantinople IV (869–70), met in relatively rapid succession, for the creed or fundamental statement of faith one council established always raised new questions that had to be addressed in turn. Some councils followed one right after the other to address the same nagging problems, with succeeding councils doing a better and more complete job than their predecessors. Four Lateran councils met successively to reform the church in 1123, 1139, 1179, and 1215. In other situations, later councils finished the work earlier ones took up but couldn't complete given difficult circumstances. This might best describe the relationship among Trent, Vatican I, and Vatican II, even though these three councils are frequently placed in opposition to one another.

This survey does not aim to give a day-to-day account of the twenty-one major councils. It will succeed if it introduces readers and students to the councils' historical contexts, major tasks, achievements and failures, and overall attempts to respond to particular and enduring challenges. Because this is a general synthesis, it does not include footnotes, but each chapter concludes with a list of specialized studies (weighted toward those in English) that formed most of the research. What I have tried to do is uncover the themes and threads that connect the twenty-one general councils while illustrating those factors, features, and contexts that made each one relatively unique.

What Is a Council?

General councils are meetings called by the pope (although this has not always been the case) whose attendees include (but are not limited to) bishops. Councils are not held according to any regular schedule, but are called as needed, so that the church as represented by the council members (often called "fathers") can address the major issues (typically religious, but sometimes political, too) of the day.

Announcing Lateran IV, for instance, Pope Innocent III declared that some very important issues were at hand. He had decided, "since these objects affect the condition of the whole body of the faithful, we should summon a general council according to the ancient custom of the holy fathers—this council to be held at a convenient time and to be concerned only with the spiritual good of souls." The pope went on to detail the council's sweeping agenda:

> ...to uproot vices and implant virtues, to correct abuses and reform morals, to eliminate heresies and strengthen faith, to allay differences and establish peace, to check persecutions and cherish liberty, to persuade Christian princes and peoples to grant succor and support for the Holy Land from both clergy and laymen, and for other reasons which it would be tedious to enumerate here.

He also instructed the archbishops and bishops, abbots and priors to whom he sent this letter to show up in Rome two and a half years after his summons. "Meantime," he instructed, "both personally and by discreet agents, you will inquire precisely about all matters which seem to call for energetic correction of reform and, conscientiously writing a report, you will deliver it for the scrutiny of the sacred council."

From the first moments of the church's life, Christians have used these types of major meetings to compare notes and solve problems. Constance (1414–18), a very controversial council that tried to put councils on a regular schedule—in large part to assert their claim to authority over the papacy—noted in 1417: "The frequent holding of general councils is a *pre-eminent* means of

4

cultivating the Lord's patrimony. It roots out the briars, thorns, and thistles of heresies, errors, and schisms; corrects deviations; reforms what is deformed; and produces a richly fertile crop for the Lord's vineyard" (emphasis added).

Although Constance failed to make the meeting of general councils common and regular, no one in the church doubted a general council's crucial importance. Five years before Luther posted his *95 Theses,* John Colet, the dean of St. Paul's Cathedral in London and a friend of Erasmus, preached a sermon to a gathering of England's clergy. Knowing the church needed to call a council to address her critical state, Colet in 1512 flatly declared: "For nothing ever happens more detrimental to the church of Christ than the omission of councils, both general and provincial."

General councils meet for a variety of reasons, and it has often been said Vatican II was the first council without a major doctrinal issue at the top of its "to-do" list. This statement may exaggerate the point, as not every council before Vatican II met primarily to address doctrine, but it is true Vatican II was a different type of council. Pope Paul VI, in his 1964 encyclical *Ecclesiam Suam,* recognized this fact when he gave the green light to Vatican II to continue its innovative actions:

> How often in past centuries has the determination to instigate reforms been associated with the holding of ecumenical councils! Let it be so once more; but this time not with a view to removing any specific heresies concerning the church or to remedying any public disorders—for disorders of this sort have not, thank God, raised their head in our midst—but rather with a view to infusing fresh spiritual vigor into Christ's mystical body considered as a visible society and to purifying it from the defects of many of its members and urging it on to the attainment of new virtue.

Paul VI was speaking about Vatican II, the twenty-first and most recent general council. What was her first?

Although the "Council of Jerusalem" is not listed among the twenty-one councils considered "general" or "ecumenical," this meeting of Peter and James, Paul and Barnabas, and others is frequently identified as the model council. Constantinople II in 553, for example, explicitly noted the importance of this example of the apostles coming together in consultation to make a decision. The New Testament offers two accounts of this meeting: Acts of the Apostles 15 and Galatians 2:1–10. This "council" probably met in 49 or 50, for less than two decades after Jesus' resurrection the question arose: "Do you have to be a Jew in order to be a Christian?" The practical issue came down to whether men required circumcision and all had to observe the Jewish dietary laws.

An element important for later councils comes up in the first few verses of Acts 15: Paul and Barnabas were "appointed to go up to Jerusalem to discuss this question with the apostles and the elders. So they were sent on their way by the church...." This key pattern repeats itself constantly: Leaders from distant and diverse settings travel to a central place as representatives of their communities to discuss a common problem and its solution. In this first case, all concerned met in Jerusalem to talk about and decide the issue. James offered a "live and let live" compromise, fundamentally saying that Gentile men need not be circumcised to be followers of Christ. Again giving an important precedent, the gathering then sent a letter detailing the decision, noting most critically the source of its authority (Acts 15:28): "For it has seemed good to the holy spirit and to us...."

In Paul's version from Galatians, the group agreed over a handshake, making it sound more like everyone participated equally. According to Acts, however, James listened to everybody and then made a decision: "My brothers, listen to me....Therefore I have reached the decision..." (Acts 15:13,19). But the use of "us" in the letter indicates that everybody present concurred with his decision. There is an apparent discrepancy between Acts, which indicates one decision maker to whom others assented, and Galatians, which sounds more like the decision was based on a consensus among those gathered. This situation illustrates a tension between popes (exercising their primacy) and bishops (emphasizing collegiality and collaborative action) that recurs several times during general councils over the centuries.

The current Code of Canon Law (1983) addressed this crucial relationship between pope and bishops at general councils. The Code described general councils and their authority, especially with reference to the pope, within a section devoted to the college of bishops (canons 336–41). This section overlaps with Vatican II's document *Lumen Gentium* (no. 22), which speaks almost the exact same language.

The Code identifies the college, along with the pope, as the final authority in the church: "The college of bishops, whose head is the Supreme Pontiff...together with its head and never without this head, is also the subject of supreme and full power over the universal church" (c. 336). Pope and bishops are knitted closely together, especially in a general council, and it must be remembered that the pope belongs to the college of bishops, too, as head of the Roman diocese. But the reiterated emphasis on the pope as "head" of the college of bishops that holds supreme authority "together with its head and never without this head" is critical.

As for councils, the Code states: "The college of bishops exercises power over the universal church in a solemn manner in an ecumenical council" (c. 337). While the pope is, in one way, only a single member of the college of bishops as a bishop himself, as pope he has sole authority in some areas: "It is for the Roman Pontiff alone to convoke an ecumenical council, preside over it personally or through others, transfer, suspend, or dissolve a council, and to approve its decrees" (c. 338). This same canon also lays down that the pope sets the council's agenda and procedures, but members can add other items as long as the pope approves them.

The current Code of Canon Law states that an ecumenical council cannot exist outside the pope's authority. During the first millennium, however, emperors and one empress called and sometimes presided over councils, although for the most part with the popes' knowledge and blessing. Moreover, popes did not always attend general councils: When they did not personally show up, they sent legates to speak in their name.

A general council's decrees are not considered binding and valid until the pope approves them and orders the documents published. The language in the Code is interesting: "The decrees of an ecumenical council do not have obligatory force unless they have been approved by the Roman Pontiff together with the council fathers, confirmed by him, and promulgated at his order" (c. 341). According to this careful wording, the pope approves the decrees with the council's members, but only the pope confirms those decrees and orders them shared with the wider church community.

But it takes more than a pope to make a general council. Bishops are the main participants, and by canon law they alone have the right to a deliberative vote: a vote that is binding on a council's decisions and not merely an opinion that can be discarded. The pope can invite other people to a council and determine how they will participate (c. 339). This happened at Vatican II, which gave a deliberative vote to the heads of religious orders and listened to the advice of many experts and observers (clerical and lay, male and female, Catholic and non-Catholic), especially in committee sessions, public lectures, and private seminars.

Until now, we have seen the words "general council" and "ecumenical council" used somewhat loosely. It is necessary to tighten their meanings as much as possible. The word *ecumenical* comes from the Greek word for "universal." Technically, an "ecumenical" council is one with representatives of the church throughout the world. Based on that definition, the first seven major councils are considered ecumenical, as Chalcedon called itself in 451. These first seven (Nicaea I in 325 to Nicaea II in 787) included bishops from the eastern and western parts of the Roman Empire (considered the "whole world" at that time), though just a few westerners were present in some of them. At Nicaea I, for example, 220 bishops participated, but only a handful were from the west. Eastern bishops made up all of Constantinople I (381) and most of Ephesus (431), Chalcedon (451), Constantinople II (553), and Constantinople III (680–81).

While the Eastern Orthodox Church considers only the first seven councils ecumenical, the Roman Catholic Church recognizes twenty-one as paramount and has called different councils "ecumenical" or "general," even though the east was missing from most general councils in the second millennium. Lateran I (1123) referred to itself as a general and not an ecumenical council, which is correct, as no eastern bishops participated. Basel-Ferrara-Florence-Rome (1431–45) accurately called itself ecumenical/universal when eastern and western bishops talked about reuniting the church.

Paul VI described Vatican II as ecumenical in *Ecclesiam Suam*, as we have already heard, and there were indeed eastern bishops present. But in 1974 when the pope recognized the seven hundredth anniversary of Lyons II (1274), he precisely said it was "counted sixth among the general synods celebrated in the western world." This makes sense when you do the math: if you reckon the first eight as ecumenical and recognize they met in cities located in the eastern half of the empire, then Lyons II was indeed the sixth of the medieval general councils, all of which took place in western Europe.

The language of "universal," "ecumenical," and "general" councils is without doubt applied imprecisely. (This book will use "general council" to acknowledge the east's absence from most meetings after the first millennium.) Moreover, the Roman church's twenty-one general councils are not designated by decree but taken by custom, sometimes over the course of time. Chalcedon (451) brought Constantinople I (381) up to the highest ranks by placing its creed on par with Nicaea I's (325). But several centuries had to pass before the west recognized Constantinople IV (869–70) along with its seven predecessors—which many in the east never did.

In addition, Paul VI's use of "synod" instead of "council" to describe Lyons II may appear confusing, but "synod" and "council" are mostly taken as the same thing in the records. What's different, however, is the distinction between general, universal, or ecumenical meetings on the one hand, and local, regional, or provincial meetings on the other. Many provincial and local councils (or synods) met during the first three centuries of the church, especially during the third century, to deal with matters of discipline and doctrine. In a sense, these early church meetings in North

Africa, Rome, Gaul, Asia Minor, and the Iberian Peninsula worked their way up to Nicaea I, the first general council. In addition, there were many local meetings, some including popes or their representatives, during the Middle Ages that are not counted with Lateran I through IV, Lyons I and II, and Vienne as medieval general councils. Regional synods of bishops continue to meet, sometimes in Rome, often by region (such as the "Synod of the Americas"), and frequently in their home countries as national synods or conferences.

Finally, the time between each of the twenty-one general councils, their duration, and their attendance have varied greatly. The number *twenty-one* at first glance leads us to believe general councils met about once each century during the church's first two millennia. In reality, general councils have met infrequently and in clusters, with long stretches that saw no general councils at all.

Christianity had to wait three centuries, until it was recognized by the Roman Empire, before it could hold its first general council. Then, eight general councils sat in the 545 years between Nicaea I (325) and Constantinople IV (869–70). More than two and a half centuries then passed before seven medieval councils met within 189 years: Lateran I (1123) to Vienne (1311–12). Another century went by before two general councils met within about three decades: Constance (1414–18) to Basel-Ferrara-Florence-Rome (1431–45). Lateran V followed more than sixty years later, then Trent met in three stages further along in the sixteenth century, concluding in 1563. Over three centuries passed before the next council sat, Vatican I (1869–70), which was itself separated by nearly a century from Vatican II (1962–65).

General councils have sat for as short as a week (Lateran II, 1139) and as long as three and a half years of fairly steady activity (Constance, 1414–18). Length of time, however, does not indicate importance or achievement. Lateran IV met for only twenty days, yet it is the most impressive of medieval reform councils. Vatican II technically sat for just 281 days spread over four autumn terms, but as at most councils, much work took place behind the scenes before and after the sessions proper. Lateran V met for nearly five full years (1512–17), yet accomplished very little.

In terms of participation, as few as a dozen members were in attendance at one point during Constantinople IV (869–70) and only seventeen during a particular session of Trent (1551–52). These numbers stand in stark contrast to the 2,540 people clogging St. Peter's Basilica during Vatican II's first session in 1962. The period of a general council did not necessarily influence attendance, either. Despite difficulties in travel and communication during the ancient and medieval eras, about six hundred people took part in Chalcedon (451), over four hundred at Lateran IV (1215), and almost nine hundred at Constance (1414–18).

Regardless of their unique qualities, general councils share a common thread: they attempt to respond to the urgent needs of their day. Having taken a broad view of conciliar history and events, it is now time to consider how each of the church's twenty-one general councils responded to its particular challenges.

BIBLIOGRAPHY

Conciliar Documents

Norman P. Tanner, ed. *Decrees of the Ecumenical Councils,* 2 vols. London: Sheed & Ward and Washington D.C.: Georgetown University Press, 1990. All quotations will come from this collection, which provides conciliar documents translated from their original languages on facing pages. The conciliar texts are reproduced from Giuseppe Alberigo, et al., eds. *Conciliorum œcumenicorum decreta.* Bologna: Istituto per le scienze religiose, 1973.

Surveys

Giuseppe Alberigo, ed. *Les Conciles Œcuméniques.* Vol. 1, *L'Histoire.* Paris: Les Éditions du Cerf, 1994.

C. J. Hefele. *Histoire des conciles d'après les documents originaux.* 11 vols. Translated and continued by H. Leclercq. Paris: Letouzey et Ané, 1907–52.

Philip Hughes. *The Church in Crisis: A History of the General Councils 325–1870.* Garden City N.Y.: Hanover House, 1961.

Peter Huizing and Knut Walf, eds. *The Ecumenical Council: Its Significance in the Constitution of the Church.* Edinburgh: T. & T. Clark, 1983 [=*Concilium,* vol. 167, July 1983].

Hubert Jedin. *Ecumenical Councils in the Catholic Church: An Historical Survey.* Translated by Ernest Graf. New York: Herder and Herder, 1960.

Norman P. Tanner. *The Councils of the Church: A Short History.* New York: The Crossroad Publishing Company, 2001.

Part I

COUNCILS IN THE FIRST MILLENNIUM

Overleaf: Colossal Bust of Constantine, Rome, Italy. Courtesy of Alinari/Art Resource, N.Y.

During the first millennium of Christianity, the church held councils on several levels: local, regional or provincial, universal or ecumenical. The Roman Catholic Church recognizes eight of the largest gatherings as the first general councils: from Nicaea I (325) to Constantinople IV (869–70).

The first six—Nicaea I to Constantinople III (680–81)—cannot be separated from one another. The challenges each of these six general councils faced flowed out of one and into the next. Church leaders gathered to accomplish a nearly impossible task: to hammer out in words the central mysteries of Jesus' humanity and divinity, of the Trinity's essence, and of Mary's relationship to Jesus as God and human being. As soon as one council made a definition of faith and proclaimed its decisions, fresh questions emerged. Every solution raised new uncertainty.

The last two general councils of the first millennium break this pattern. Nicaea II (787) largely addressed iconoclasm, an issue of worship with theological underpinnings. Constantinople IV (869–70) dealt more with church structures, procedures, and internal politics than anything else. These two councils stand apart from the prior six.

Most of these first eight general councils also discussed disciplinary issues: the reception of penitent heretics, the election of bishops, episcopal jurisdiction and independence, the role secular people played in church matters, the moral (and immoral) behavior of the clergy, the correction of worldliness and greed, and the need for frequent provincial synods to deal with the regular and extraordinary business of a church that was expanding and organizing herself.

Chapter 1
Developing Doctrine: Nicaea I (325) to Constantinople III (680–681)

The church waited nearly three centuries after the "Council of Jerusalem" (ca. 50) to call her first general council. This delay occurred largely because Christianity was still officially outlawed until Constantine legitimated the faith: As Roman emperor, he allowed Christians freedom to worship with the Edict of Milan in 313. But there were questions deeply dividing this new faith. Constantine did not wish to see Christianity work against his empire's unity and peace; indeed, he may have chosen to favor Christianity because he believed this faith, unlike paganism, would help fuse the Roman Empire into one solid community.

The spark of division was the theology proposed by Arius, a priest who emphasized Jesus' humanity at the expense of his divinity. Over the next 350 years, others built on Arius's theological starting point, applying the principle to related questions of Christology and Trinitarian theology. In response, theologians opposing Arius and his followers strongly defended Jesus' divinity, but they sometimes erred in the opposite direction: They intently focused on Jesus' divinity, at times to the prejudice of his humanity. The resulting series of arguments and counter-arguments provided the impetus that led one general council to follow its predecessor in turn from Nicaea I (325) to Constantinople III (680–81).

Nicaea I

In the first attempt to settle the dispute concerning Arius's position, and thereby bring social and religious peace, Constantine called the empire's bishops together at Nicaea I. He exerted strong leadership at this first general council: Not only did the emperor summon the meeting, but he initially presided over it, held the gathering in his own palace (in present-day Turkey), addressed the members, and at the meeting's conclusion confirmed and then promulgated its decrees. The pope, Silvester I, did not attend but sent two legates in his name. This precedent of imperial oversight would distinguish many of the other general councils during the church's first millennium.

The first general council emerged from events preceding it. This "cause-and-effect" relationship set up a blueprint subsequent general councils would often follow. Arius had for some time taught that Jesus was not eternal and uncreated like God the Father. To the consternation of his bishop, Alexander, Arius preached that "there was a time when [Jesus] was not" in existence. This principle had theological implications, for if Jesus were not coeternal with the Father, then he must have been created by the Father, and therefore he must be God's inferior. Even if Jesus had been the most superior human being, he could not have been divine unless God the Father had adopted him, which still would not bring Jesus' divine nature up to par with the Father's. By extension, the Holy Spirit would have been even less divine than Jesus. Arian theology drew one more troubling conclusion: If only God can save human beings, and Jesus is not God, then Jesus did not save human beings.

Alexander and about a hundred bishops rebuked Arius, excommunicating and exiling him in a synod held in North Africa about 320. This action did not stop Arius, whose followers held their own synod to counter Alexander's. After a few more local councils in 324 and 325, Constantine held his general council to settle the matter at Nicaea I, which drew between 220 and 250 bishops. Tradition claims 318 bishops attended, following the number of Abraham's assistants (Gen 14:14); later councils like Chalcedon referred to the faith professed by the 318 at Nicaea I. Nearly all of these bishops were from the eastern half of the Roman Empire.

About a dozen Arian bishops attended Nicaea I, but a large majority of other bishops rejected their presentation of the Christian faith. Led by Bishop Alexander's deacon, Athanasius (who later succeeded him as bishop of Alexandria), the gathering produced a statement that, among other things, dealt specifically with Jesus' equality with his Father. The council eventually used the word *homo-ousios* to define the fact that Jesus is "one in being" or "of the same being" or "of the same substance" as his Father. Jesus was not made and therefore was not a creature of a creator. The council taught that the Son is the Father's coequal, is coeternal with the Father, and is begotten (not made) of the same substance as the Father. The council added to its profession of faith twenty disciplinary canons and a letter explaining its actions to the church in Egypt.

Controversy persisted, however, and this unsteady fallout from the council of Nicaea I was simply one more "first" in a pattern connected to almost all of the twenty-one general councils. No matter how clear their statements, general councils and their actions often encountered obstacles after they concluded. A particularly strange turn of events occurred after Nicaea I. Because of a complicated set of religious and political rivalries, some groups praised the condemned heretic Arius as a hero while Athanasius found himself exiled several times from his episcopal seat at Alexandria. At one point Constantine himself, who oversaw Arius's defeat at Nicaea I in large part because of Athanasius's work, exiled Athanasius all the way to Trier in modern-day Germany.

Nicaea I's creed answered some questions, but unintentionally raised new ones about Christology and Trinitarian theology. What about the Holy Spirit and its relationship to Father and Son? If Jesus was fully divine and divinity is superior to humanity, was Jesus' humanity eaten up by his divinity? These questions were exacerbated by the fact that, despite the Nicene condemnations, Arianism persisted—so much so that Jerome, the translator of the Bible into Latin, complained forty years after Nicaea I, "The whole world groaned to find itself Arian."

Theological language and technical vocabulary became a troublesome issue for the fourth-century councils. After Nicaea I, theologians worked to find words to express a mystery: Jesus is at the same time human and divine. Moreover, he is *fully* human and *fully* divine, but still only one person, not two separate people. In addition, Nicaea I did not completely explain how God could have one unified nature while at the same time be God in three distinct persons: Father, Son, Spirit. So a major hurdle existed from the very beginning: Flawed humans attempted to use imprecise language to define what ultimately cannot be explained in human terms.

On top of that, the east quite literally spoke one language (Greek) while the west spoke another (Latin). Each language had its own nuances that could not be translated exactly into the other. Not every eastern bishop and theologian who spoke Greek could fluently comprehend and speak Latin, and vice versa. At times, the east and the west spoke at or past each other, not with each other. True dialogue could not take place. (A modern example might be the way diplomats wearing headsets at United Nations debates sometimes miss the subtleties of a treaty's phrasing because there is no precise counterpart in German, say, for a word in Chinese.)

Despite Nicaea I, Arians continued to assert Jesus was not completely divine. Some of them, known as semi-Arians, took the word *homo-ousios* and, using another Greek term, added an "i" to make it *homoi-ousios* to describe Jesus as similar (but not the same) in being with the father. For these semi-Arians, Jesus was "like" God, but not God. Other heresies followed Nicaea I. One group denied the Holy Spirit was divine, drawing this conclusion from Arius's position that Jesus was not divine. To fight these heresies, a theologian named Apollinaris stressed Jesus' divinity so much he ended up asserting Jesus was fully divine but not fully human. Even the defenders of Nicaea I ended up stumbling away from orthodoxy.

Constantinople I

Clearly Nicaea I had not entirely settled the issue, which made another council necessary. The emperor Theodosius the Great pictured himself in the mold of Constantine: defender of the faith. While Constantine's Edict of Milan had tolerated Christianity, in 380 and 381 Theodosius made Christianity the only legal faith in the Roman Empire, branding as heresies all other ideas not in conformity with "the faith of Nicaea." As part of his attempt to achieve unity and peace, Theodosius called a second general council, a step many bishops had asked him to take. After this meeting and at the request of the bishops, Theodosius approved and then promulgated their documents. No decrees from the 381 meeting have survived, but we do have a letter from a synod held in Constantinople the following year that relates the 381 meeting's actions and statements.

The fathers at Constantinople I (present-day Istanbul) knew that Arians endured, even flourished, regardless of Nicaea I's actions. Their very persistence, in fact, is one reason why this general council picked up where its predecessor had left off. Constantinople I reaffirmed the Nicene creed while moving the Holy Spirit closer to the idea of *homo-ousios*. In 325, the Nicene fathers had said only that they believed in the Holy Spirit, without applying any of the language used to describe the Father's relationship with the Son to the Spirit. Constantinople I put the Holy Spirit on the same level as God the Father and Son. The bishops at Constantinople I proclaimed they believed "in the spirit, the holy, the lordly and life-giving one, proceeding forth from the father, co-worshipped and co-glorified with father and son."

No western bishops attended Constantinople I in 381, and Pope Damasus I did not send delegates, but this council is now indisputably considered by both east and west as ecumenical. This was not always the case. Some objected at the time to the designation "ecumenical," which the council apparently used to describe itself. The letter from 382 details for the pope what actions Constantinople I took, but we do not know if the pope accepted them in his own synod at Rome that year.

Ephesus

After Constantinople I, Christological questions continued to arise. How was Jesus one person, both human and divine? Was he really two separate people at the same time he was also one merged person? Was he sometimes human and at other times divine? What were the consequences of these answers for Mary and the incarnation? Was she the mother of the human Jesus only (known therefore as *christotokos*) or was she the mother of God (making her *theotokos*)? It would take another council, this one at Ephesus (in modern Turkey) in 431, to deal with these subjects.

The leading protoganist of the new debate was Nestorius. Ironically, as bishop of Constantinople, Nestorius tried to wipe out any persisting adherents of Arianism and its polar opposite, Apollinarianism. Nestorius taught that Mary was the mother of the human being Jesus but not the mother of God. Others pushed the idea, proposing Jesus was two separate people ("other and other"): The Jesus with a divine nature was the Son of God, and the Jesus with a human nature was the son of Mary. Cyril of Alexandria, a follower of Athanasius, became Nestorianism's chief opponent, and the pope, Celestine, allowed Cyril to speak for him. Cyril argued that Nestorianism split Jesus in half, denying that the human and divine Jesus were one and the same person.

After local synods debated the matter and condemned Nestorius, a process that repeated what had occurred with Arius before Nicaea I, the emperor Theodosius II called the third general council— the most raucous and confused to date. Although it was Nestorius who had pressed the emperor for a general council, the pope agreed a council was necessary. Cyril presided at Ephesus in 431 and oversaw the condemnation of Nestorius; the council members then sent a letter to Nestorius calling him "a new Judas." According to Cyril, the people of Ephesus danced in the streets and paraded with torches in joy. As far as he was concerned, the matter was settled.

However, Cyril had begun the council proceedings before most of the eastern bishops who backed Nestorius and even the pope's legates had arrived. The eastern bishops, led by John of Antioch, appeared a few days later. When they discovered what Cyril had done without them, they held a competing council, which condemned Cyril. Then Celestine's delegates arrived: Once they found out about the two "councils," they met with Cyril, supported his condemnation of Nestorius, and added their own of John of Antioch and his group. Several weeks later, Theodosius II, who had not wanted Cyril to begin before all parties were present, condemned everyone and told them to leave. Both sides subsequently tried to get the emperor to back their position, but there were no clear winners as the delegates departed.

Cyril triumphed over time. About two years later, John and Cyril negotiated a truce that basically represented the final victory of Cyril's positions. The eastern bishops condemned Nestorius, recognized Mary as *theotokos* (mother of God), and said Jesus indeed had a human and divine nature united in only one person. The new pope, Sixtus III, sent letters to Cyril and John acknowledging their agreement. In 436, the emperor exiled Nestorius and ordered all of his writings burned. Sixtus III, and later the general council of Chalcedon (451), recognized the meetings held under Cyril and the papal legates, not those led by John of Antioch, as the authentic council of Ephesus.

Ephesus is important from a doctrinal standpoint because it explained the "hypostatic union" by which Jesus' human and divine natures are fused into one person. Among the council's documents is a letter, the second letter Cyril sent to Nestorius. In it, Cyril explains this fundamental theological point, which required further explication after Nicaea I and Constantinople I.

...[W]e do not say that the nature of the Word was changed and became flesh, nor that he was turned into a whole man made of body and soul. Rather do we claim that the Word in an unspeakable, inconceivable manner united to himself hypostatically flesh enlivened by a rational soul, and so became man and was called son of man, not by God's will alone or good pleasure, nor by the assumption of a person alone. Rather did two different natures come together to form a unity, and from both arose one Christ, one Son. It was not as though the distinctness of the natures was destroyed by the union, but divinity and humanity together made perfect for us one Lord and one Christ, together marvelously and mysteriously combining to form a unity.

Cyril made clear Jesus is one person with two natures and the divine nature did not overwhelm the human nature. But this raised another question: If humanity and divinity are together in one person, did divinity suffer and die? This time, the next logical question did not have to wait decades for another council's answer. Just a few sentences later, Cyril explained:

...[W]e say that he suffered and rose again, not that the Word of God suffered blows or piercing with nails or any other wounds in his own nature (for the divine, being without a body, is incapable of suffering); but because the body which became his own suffered these things, he is said to have suffered them for us.

Jesus' human nature suffered because it is human and therefore capable of suffering; his divine nature did not suffer because it could not suffer.

In its letter informing all concerned about the condemnations, Cyril's meeting referred to itself as orthodox and ecumenical. It repeated the Nicene definition of faith and then asserted, "It is not permitted to produce or write or compose any other creed except the one which was defined by the holy fathers who were gathered together in the holy spirit at Nicaea." When Cyril wrote to John to settle their differences, he again stressed Nicaea I's preeminence:

We do not permit anyone in any way to upset the defined faith or the creed drawn up by the holy fathers who assembled at Nicaea as the times demanded. We give neither ourselves nor them the license to alter any expression there or to change a single syllable, remembering the words: "Remove not the ancient landmarks which your fathers have set" (Prv 22:28).

Chalcedon

Despite these warnings about not altering any expressions of the faith, the church had to explain these theological points a bit more fully at yet another general council, which had to meet only two decades later. Chalcedon tried to summarize all the confusion, explanation, and counter-explanation of the 125 years since Nicaea I. Even with the statements made by Nicaea I, Constantinople I, and Ephesus in hand, some theologians still had difficulty striking a balance of Christological language and ideas.

One group, for example, continued to emphasize Jesus' divinity. In the tradition of Apollinarianism, some taught Jesus' divine nature overwhelmed and, in a sense, canceled out his human nature. This idea, known as monophysitism (one nature), found a champion in Eutyches, a monk living in Constantinople.

Chalcedon had a difficult start. Two years earlier, Pope Leo I's representatives had attended a meeting in Ephesus, but three times some participants blocked the papal legates from reading aloud Leo's statement of faith addressing monophysitism (his *Tome*). A near-riot broke out and soldiers cleared the basilica. Naturally, Leo I did not recognize this meeting as a legitimate council. He declared it had not been a judgment but a robbery, and because of his statement this meeting came to be known as the "Robber Synod."

After this fractured meeting, the emperor Theodosius II tried to call a general council to settle the matter. Leo wanted this council to meet in Italy, but eventually Theodosius II's successor, Marcian, called the meeting for Chalcedon (another city in modern Turkey) in 451. Pope Leo I again sent delegates and his *Tome*. Although only about a half-dozen westerners attended Chalcedon, the papal legates dominated the discussion. By the meeting's conclusion, the fathers were shouting their agreement with the *Tome* by acclaiming: "Peter has spoken through Leo!" Marcian immediately confirmed Chalcedon's work, but the members also asked Leo to approve the council's documents, which the pope did (except for one major issue, to be treated later in this chapter) after close review two years later.

The major doctrinal statement by Chalcedon reasserted a fundamental Christian mystery: Jesus is one person with two natures joined together in a hypostatic union. These two natures were separate and equal: The divine nature did not overwhelm the human. After repeating the creeds of Nicaea I and Constantinople I, which they professed to follow, the council fathers at Chalcedon reviewed, reiterated, and delineated nearly four centuries of theology about Jesus.

> ...[W]e all with one voice teach the confession of one and the same son, our Lord Jesus Christ: the same perfect in divinity and perfect in humanity, the same truly God and truly man, of a rational soul and a body; consubstantial with the father as regards his divinity, and the same consubstantial with us as regards his humanity; like us in all respects except for sin; begotten before the ages from the father as regards his divinity, and in the last days the same for us and for our salvation from Mary, the virgin God-bearer, as regards his humanity; one and the same Christ, son, Lord, only-begotten, acknowledged in two natures which undergo no confusion, no change, no division, no separation; at no point was the difference between the natures taken away through the union, but rather the property of both natures is preserved and comes together into a single person and a single subsistent being; he is not parted or divided into two persons, but is one and the same only-begotten son, God, Word, Lord Jesus Christ....

The Chalcedon fathers believed the case was finally closed:

> Since we have formulated these things with all possible accuracy and attention, the sacred and universal synod decreed that no one is permitted to produce, or even to write down or compose, any other creed or to think or teach otherwise.

Chalcedon offers another reminder of how one council builds on another. The bishops at Chalcedon explicitly noted their adherence to the creeds of the traditional "318" fathers at Nicaea I and the "150" at Constantinople I, Cyril's second letter to Nestorius (part of Ephesus's documents), and Leo's *Tome* (included with Chalcedon's). Nicaea I, Constantinople I, Ephesus, and Chalcedon were emerging as preeminent and more significant than the local and regional synods that worked out doctrinal language before and between these four general councils. In fact, Pope Gregory I (590–604) declared these first four general councils to be as authoritative as the four gospels.

Constantinople II

Even with such authoritative declarations of the orthodox faith, Nestorianism lingered, and in 553 the emperor Justinian called another general council, Constantinople II. The combination of a weak pope and extremely complex politics in Justinian's Byzantine court made its meetings very complicated.

Justinian wanted Constantinople II to condemn the writings of three men (Theodore of Mopsuestia, Theodoret of Cyr, and Ibas of Edessa) whose individual statements were grouped together as the "three chapters." These writers were accused of being sympathetic with Nestorianism, of opposing Cyril's teaching, and of favoring monophysitism by clinging to the idea Jesus had one nature, with the divine overpowering the human.

The pope, Vigilius, did not attend the council, though he was in Constantinople at the time. He was an ambitious man who had been in league with the empress Theodora, Justinian's formidable wife. Though dead by the time Constantinople II met, Theodora had favored monophysitism and over a decade earlier had helped get Vigilius elected pope with his promise to deny Chalcedon's teachings on Jesus' natures and personhood. The pope could not easily abandon Chalcedon, although Vigilius may have privately indicated he agreed with the monophysites. He seems to have played both sides, however: Several times he wrote to Justinian saying he would indeed support Chalcedon against mono-physitism. Meanwhile, Theodora died in 548, making it easier for Justinian to move against the monophysites and Nestorianism more vigorously.

Justinian led Constantinople II without Vigilius. The emperor oversaw the condemnation of the person and the writings of Theodore of Mopsuestia, the writings (but not the person) of Theodoret of Cyr, and the letter attributed to Ibas of Edessa; Ibas himself was not condemned because the council decided he had not written the letter in question. Vigilius refused to comply with the condemnations, which proved embarrassing for him when Justinian produced letters the pope had written to the emperor promising to join in censuring the three chapters. Treated roughly by the emperor, the pope finally relented and went along with Constantinople II's actions, claiming he had rethought his earlier sympathies for the monophysites.

Politics aside, Constantinople II clarified yet again the church's teaching on Jesus' two natures united hypostatically in his one person. In very harsh tones, this general council condemned previous heretical doctrines on the subject and issued fourteen anathemas against them. These constitute a handy synopsis of Christology, Mariology, and Trinitarian theology to date. The fathers censured not only the heretics but those who allowed heresy to persist. More positively, they confessed as orthodox the faith of Nicaea I, Constantinople I, Ephesus, and Chalcedon, providing additional prestige to these first four general councils as the pillars of early church dogma.

Constantinople III

There was one more Christological battle left to fight: If Jesus is one person with two natures (one human and one divine), how many wills does he have? Chalcedon, which seemed to have answered all the questions with its precise words, did not deal clearly enough with this aspect of Christology for some theologians. Over time, a school of thinkers declared Jesus has only one will. This heresy, monothelitism, merged the human will of Jesus' human nature with the divine will of Jesus' divine nature.

In response to monothelitism, a familiar pattern repeated itself. The pope, Agatho, called for local synods to address the matter; we know for sure some met in Milan and England. Then the pope called a Roman synod to consider what the local synods had to say. Finally, Agatho with Emperor Constantine IV decided it would take yet another general council, Constantinople III (680–81), to settle the matter definitively.

Constantinople III, like most councils of the first millennium, was comprised mainly of easterners, but the west exerted significant influence. The council condemned monothelitism, declaring that Jesus, who is one person, has two wills (one human and one divine), which match his human and divine natures. The fathers expressly noted that their council, "in its turn under God's inspiration," was only following the tradition recognized at Nicaea I in 325 and supported through the next four general councils. They approved Pope Agatho's report on monothelitism from his Roman synod and placed it on the same level of prestige as Cyril's letters against Nestorius and Leo I's *Tome*.

Constantinople III's own words provide evidence that general councils do not always lay problems to rest. The fathers lamented that, despite the five prior councils' professions of faith and condemnations of heresy, trouble had still been at work, which explained why they had been forced to meet. After repeating verbatim the creeds of Nicaea I and Constantinople I, the fathers remarked:

> This pious and orthodox creed of the divine favor was enough for a complete knowledge of the orthodox faith and a complete assurance therein. But since, from the first, the contriver of evil did not rest, finding an accomplice in the serpent and through him bringing upon human nature the poisoned dart of death, so too now he has found instruments suited to his own purpose...and has not been idle in raising through them obstacles of error against the full body of the church....

Because of its statement against monothelitism, this council (which had papal support and included Agatho's legates) had to condemn a prior pope, Honorius I (625–38), who believed Jesus has only one will. Later, some would interpret Honorius I as a well-meaning but misguided pope; as a pope who did not really hold a heretical position, but who did not do enough to fight it; or as a man who made a mistake as an individual believer that did not compromise the church's doctrinal infallibility. The emperor and the next pope, Leo II, approved Constantinople III's statements; Leo II also declared Constantinople III ecumenical, but the fathers had already done that for themselves.

Chapter 2
Prayer and Politics: Nicaea II (787) and Constantinople IV (869–870)

The first six general councils had largely settled the early church's main questions concerning Christology, Mariology, and Trinitarian theology. Versions of the core heresies from Christianity's first six centuries would continually resurface, but the church's responses to these challenges had pretty much played themselves out by Constantinople III. The first millennium would witness two more general councils, which wrapped politics and religion together.

Nicaea II

The seventh general council, Nicaea II in 787, met to discuss a very contentious liturgical issue: whether or not the faithful should venerate icons of Jesus, Mary, and the saints. This debate on iconoclasm consumed the eastern empire. Monks, government officials, and soldiers led the attack on icon veneration. Although it is unclear why iconoclasm developed, it appears those first opposing icons were latter-day monophysites who overemphasized Jesus' divinity against his humanity. They believed an image could never adequately or accurately capture Jesus' divinity. They made the additional argument that since an icon could only represent Jesus the human being, it was necessarily heretical. In general, iconoclasts considered pictures of Jesus, Mary, and the saints idolatrous and cited the Old Testament rule against false images as a precedent.

The Byzantine empress Irene, acting as regent for her young son Constantine VI, called Nicaea II to approve the use of icons. Pope Adrian I agreed that a general council was required to deal with the violence this question had generated for several decades, and he dispatched legates to Nicaea II. Under the leadership of Irene, who addressed the fathers, this general council reaffirmed the use of icons and, by extension, the church's traditional teaching that dead saints intercede on behalf of living Christians. Nicaea II, like other councils before it, stressed its continuity with the tradition of prior general councils and their statements of faith.

Nicaea II declared "the production of representational art" to be "quite in harmony with the history of the spread of the gospel." Having approved images, the councils fathers explained why they were helpful in worship and how the faithful should use them properly.

> The more frequently they are seen in representational art, the more are those who see them drawn to remember and long for those who serve as models, and to pay these images the tribute of salutation and respectful veneration. Certainly this is not the full adoration in accordance with our faith, which is properly paid only to the divine nature, but it resembles that given to the figure of the honored and life-giving cross, and also to the holy books of the gospels and to other sacred cult objects. Further, people are drawn to honor these images with the offering of incense and lights, as was piously established by ancient custom. Indeed, the honor paid to an image traverses it, reaching the model; and he who venerates the image, venerates the person represented in that image.

Nicaea II also issued four anathemas against the iconoclasts and ordered martyrs' relics installed in those churches the iconoclasts, because of their beliefs, had consecrated without them. To make sure the faithful clearly understood that the iconoclasts' ideas were heretical and to guard against the spread of these ideas, the council had all books written against icons and their veneration gathered up and locked away in Constantinople.

Constantinople IV

The final council of the first millennium was Constantinople IV in 869–70. This eighth general council dealt with doctrine only by recapitulating the actions and statements of the previous seven. Complicated power politics dominated Constantinople IV, something like the situation that had occurred at Constantinople II with Pope Vigilius and his shifting loyalties.

Although Constantinople and Rome competed for centuries, the immediate east-west tension that Emperor Basil I wanted to heal at Constantinople IV had been simmering for only a decade. Two men, Photius and Ignatius, claimed to be the legitimate patriarch of Constantinople. Pope Nicholas I had intervened in the situation, an action some in Constantinople interpreted as western interference, but which the pope saw as a legitimate exercise of his universal jurisdiction. Nicholas's legates had approved Photius's claim, but several years later the pope overrode them, excommunicated Photius, and said Ignatius should be patriarch of Constantinople. The east rejected the pope's decision and Photius, in his 867 synod, declared Pope Nicholas I anathema. Meanwhile, Basil I murdered his coemperor Michael III, deposed Photius, and once more put Ignatius in as patriarch.

Basil then asked the new pope, Adrian II, to join him in a council. Constantinople IV approved Photius's deposition, condemned him, and burned the writings connected to his actions in 867 against the papacy. It declared its opposition to clerics whom Photius had ordained and promoted, then ordered their churches and altars reconsecrated. The council also rehabilitated the deceased

Pope Nicholas I by honoring him and recognizing his actions. These moves not only restored Nicholas's honor, but also gave great prestige to the papacy. Ironically, this support for Rome occurred in Constantinople, whose patriarch and own high standing represented serious challenges to papal primacy and supremacy during Christianity's first millennium.

Because of its unabashed power politics and the role personalities played, Constantinople IV may be the least impressive of the first cluster of general councils—indeed of all the twenty-one general councils taken together. The next pope, John VIII, apparently went so far as to reject Constantinople IV when writing to Photius, who had regained his position as patriarch of Constantinople when Ignatius died. Although the written record is inconclusive, according to an important medieval canonist, "The synod of Constantinople which was held against Photius must not be recognized. John VIII wrote to the patriarch Photius [in 879]: 'We make void that synod which was held against Photius at Constantinople and we have completely blotted it out for various reasons as well as for the fact that Pope Adrian did not sign its acts.'" This same canonist reported that John VIII declared: "...as regards the synods which were held against Photius under Pope Adrian at Rome or Constantinople, we annul them and wholly exclude them from the number of the holy synods."

Several centuries passed before the west recognized Constantinople IV as ecumenical and placed it with the prior seven general councils. Most eastern churches still do not accept Constantinople IV as ecumenical; they replace it with another held in 879 over which Photius, restored to his see, presided. Many in the east consider the 879 council at Constantinople, not the 869–70 meeting, as the true eighth ecumenical council or at least a synod of unity.

Chapter 3
Supervising the
Early Church:
Disciplinary Canons

General councils not only defined doctrine; they also treated the procedures of the growing church. Except for Constantinople II and III, the first millennium's general councils addressed a variety of important aspects of church life in their "disciplinary canons." Often, later councils reiterated earlier councils' canons, demonstrating once more how one council rested on another for authority—but also indicating that problems persisted in spite of conciliar legislation.

Returning Heretics

The initial disciplinary issue emerged logically from the definition of orthodox faith: How would the church receive repentant heretics back into communion? The first three general councils laid down procedures for readmittance. Nicaea I declared, "...though they do not deserve leniency, nevertheless they should be treated mercifully." Nicaea I's idea of mercy surely strikes modern ears as extremely harsh: Its three-step program for readmittance totaled twelve years of penance.

Constantinople I also addressed the issue, although this canon might date not to the 381 meeting but to the 382 synod that reported its actions. The "lapsed" who had fallen away from the true faith but who now wanted to return had to produce written statements denying heretical positions. A church minister then anointed the returning Christian's forehead, eyes, nostrils, mouth, and ears with chrism, saying, "Seal of the gift of the Holy Spirit." Ephesus additionally required a signed statement agreeing with anathemas against heretical positions.

Regular Meetings

General councils recognized that they were the culmination of prior local and regional meetings; they also knew their statements needed implementation throughout the church's body. The council fathers therefore repeatedly decreed that smaller synods should meet twice each year to check on a region's ecclesiastical orthodoxy and to conduct necessary business. Nicaea I called for one provincial synod of an area's bishops before Lent and a second in autumn, specifically to inquire about cases of excommunication. Constantinople I reminded everyone of Nicaea I's canon on this item.

But Chalcedon in 451 reported Nicaea I's requirement from 325 was not being kept: "[A]s a result, many ecclesiastical matters that need putting right are being neglected." It reiterated the requirement of twice-a-year provincial synods and mandated all bishops who failed to attend without a good excuse "to be fraternally rebuked." Nicaea II pulled back a bit from Nicaea I's requirement of two synods per year. Citing the difficulty of travel because of dangerous times or cost, this council decided only one synod per year would do. Constantinople IV considered patriarchal synods even more important than provincial synods; unlike Nicaea II, Constantinople IV did not care that attending multiple meetings might prove burdensome. The fathers at Constantinople IV considered a patriarch's council so important that they stated a bishop was to be declared deposed, defrocked, and excommunicated if he missed it without permission or an appropriate reason.

Worldliness

After Roman emperors favored Christianity in the fourth century, the church became increasingly involved in secular matters. As a result, problems of worldliness and greed began to wound the church's body. Chalcedon warned monks and clerics away from business matters. The fathers protested that clerics "are, for sordid gain, acting as hired managers of other people's property, and are involving themselves in worldly business, neglecting the service of God...." Nicaea II repeated the admonition against secular involvement by clerics, "since they are forbidden to do so by the sacred canons." Instead, Nicaea II redirected the cleric's energies: "[L]et him busy himself with the teaching of the children and servants, lecturing them on the divine scriptures, because it is for such activity that he received the priesthood." Constantinople IV reaffirmed the dangers of worldly matters, prohibiting the managers of aristocrats' homes or estates from joining the clergy of Constantinople.

Another "worldly" concern dealt with priests who were married or lived with women, the latter practice known as concubinage. Nicaea I forbade any member of the clergy from living with a woman, "with the exception of course of his mother or sister or aunt, or of any person who is above suspicion." Nicaea II over 450 years later declared a woman could not live in a bishop's house or a male monastery, as this caused scandal. This council also prohibited the establishment of new double monasteries: a single structure with nuns on one side separated from monks on the other. The fathers declared this situation to be "a cause of scandal and a stumbling block for ordinary folk."

Councils also complained about simony: the buying and selling of church positions. Chalcedon was the first to protest against people purchasing or peddling ordinations, which put both the bishop and the man being ordained on the wrong side of church law. Those found guilty lost their positions. Nicaea II forbade bishops from claiming money from their subordinates. Twice citing Chalcedon's canon as precedent, Nicaea II required the demotion of anyone guilty of simony. Offshoots of simony were pluralism, when a man would buy many offices, and then absenteeism, since he could not be present in all jobs at once. These problems are especially identified with the medieval church, but they challenged general councils starting with Chalcedon in 451. Chalcedon twice declared no cleric could hold an appointment in more than one city at a time. Nicaea II repeated this rule, saying pluralism "savors of commerce and sordid profit-making."

Bishops

Council fathers repeatedly focused on bishops' jurisdiction, independence, and mutual respect, as well as their dignity in relation to secular authority.

Nicaea I in two canons ruled against bishops, priests, and deacons who jumped from their home church (or diocese) to another without permission. Constantinople I protected each bishop's sphere of influence: "Diocesan bishops are not to intrude in churches beyond their own boundaries....Unless invited, bishops are not to go outside their diocese to perform an ordination or any other ecclesiastical business." Ephesus stated no bishop may assume oversight of another province if he or his predecessors never had such authority.

Bishops' rights and authority particularly concerned Chalcedon. The council placed monasteries under the nearby bishop's authority and assigned to bishops the management of clerics who supervised almshouses, monasteries, and shrines in their territory. Chalcedon mandated clerics must first bring legal cases before their bishop, not secular authorities. This council also made provisions for such suits to be handled on several levels, but all of them were within the church so she could judge cases on her own terms and not abdicate her legal autonomy. When treating wandering clerics, Chalcedon reiterated Nicaea I's prohibition against clerics moving on their own from one church to another but added a sentence concerned with episcopal rights. If a bishop accepted a wandering cleric, he violated the original bishop's authority; as penalty, Chalcedon declared both that second bishop and the wandering cleric excommunicated.

General councils continually affirmed each bishop's relative independence as well as the bond between each bishop and his subordinates. Nicaea II repeated that clerics could not unilaterally leave one diocese for another. Constantinople IV said any cleric, monk, or layperson who wanted to leave his bishop could do so only after "a careful inquiry and judgment in synod." No bishop could give away what belonged to another bishop or install priests in another bishop's church.

Constantinople IV used some startling examples to preserve episcopal dignity and authority. Bishops who had to meet a high military or government official must not do so "a long way from their churches, nor should they dismount from their horses or mules a long way off or bow down in fear and trembling and prostrate themselves." The council told bishops they must assert the church's ultimate authority:

> Thus the bishop will have the courage to reprimand generals and other leading officials and all other secular authorities as often as he finds them doing something unjust or unreasonable, and in this way to correct them and make them better.

Constantinople IV also condemned as crimes the rumored practice whereby government officials played dress-up as priests and bishops, held mock heresy trials and episcopal consecrations, and generally ridiculed the clergy. The council condemned all those who might take part in or fail to report these spectacles, even if they were emperors or patriarchs.

The councils in their canons also discussed the election of bishops; what sort of men should be chosen; and the need to prevent government and lay interference in the free election of bishops, a point that would have major importance in medieval general councils.

Nicaea I declared a bishop should be elected by all the bishops from a province. Those who cannot show up should provide a written vote, and at least three bishops should then ordain their new colleague. Nicaea II wanted learned and holy bishops, stipulating that a candidate

> should have a thorough knowledge of the psalter, in order that he may instruct all the clergy subordinate to him to be initiated in that book. He should also be examined without fail by the metropolitan to see if he is willing to acquire knowledge—a knowledge that should be searching and not superficial—of the sacred canons, the holy gospel, the book of the divine apostle, and all divine scripture; also if he is willing to conduct himself and teach the people entrusted to him according to the divine commandments....If someone is doubtful and ill at ease with such conduct and teaching, let him not be ordained [bishop].

Nicaea II declared invalid an episcopal election done by civil rulers, quoting verbatim Nicaea I's canon on the free election of a bishop by bishops.

General councils did not want lay elites to have a hand in internal church matters. Chalcedon complained civil authorities had split some provinces in half. Constantinople IV expressly disapproved of lay meddling in clerical advancement through holy orders and episcopal elections, and censured attempts to discredit or overthrow bishops. In a canon that proved influential in medieval discussions of church freedom, Constantinople IV declared very clearly an ancient principle.

> ...[T]he promotion and consecration of bishops should be done by means of an election and decision of the college of bishops. So [this general council] promulgates as law that no lay authority or ruler may intervene in the election or promotion of a patriarch, a metropolitan or any bishop...since it is wrong for any ruler or other lay person to have any influence in such matters....If any secular authority or ruler, or a lay person of any other status, attempts to act against the common, agreed, and canonical method of election in the church, let him be anathema.

The Pope

Finally, the councils treated a topic that would help split east and west: the relationship of the bishop of Rome to other bishops, especially the bishop of Constantinople.

The fourth-century emperor Constantine, who had favored Christianity, moved the imperial capital to Constantinople from its traditional home, the city of Rome. Constantinople grew in prestige, especially after the city of Rome fell under a series of attacks over the next several centuries. The western emperor and empire continually lost out in power and prestige to the east. Consequently, the specific power and prestige of the bishop of Constantinople began to rival that of the bishop of Rome. Some bishops of Constantinople, with eastern support, had tried to place their see just below Rome in terms of authority, but still above all of the Christian world's other bishops.

Constantinople I in 381 attempted to recognize the changing state of affairs in its canon 3, which read: "Because [Constantinople] is new Rome, the bishop of Constantinople is to enjoy the privileges of honor after the bishop of Rome." Less than a century later, Chalcedon's fathers agreed. Chalcedon in its canon 28 stated Constantinople I had

> rightly accorded prerogatives to the see of older Rome, since that is an imperial city; and moved by the same purpose, the 150 most devout bishops [at Constantinople I] apportioned equal prerogatives to the most holy see of new Rome [Constantinople], reasonably judging that the city which is honored by the imperial power and senate and enjoying privileges equaling older imperial Rome, should also be elevated to her level in ecclesiastical affairs and take second place after her.

Pope Leo I simply refused to accept canon 28. Leo believed that a pope could reject a particular canon from a general council since he was pope and had ultimate authority in ecclesiastical matters on earth. The east said he could not, because the canon had been set by all the bishops together in an ecumenical council, which to them was the highest authority in the church. According to the east, no single bishop, not even the bishop of Rome, could unilaterally change or annul a statement to which all had agreed. Once more, east and west talked past each other.

The split between east and west predated the councils, but was in some ways exacerbated by them. The power struggles behind Constantinople I's canon 3, Chalcedon's canon 28, and Leo I's dismissal of canon 28 were only steps in an ongoing rift. The flip-flopping of Pope Vigilius at Constantinople II, the condemnation of Pope Honorius at Constantinople III, and the complex political and religious shifting before, during, and after Constantinople IV certainly did not help.

What the Roman bishop saw as the legitimate exercise of Peter's power of the keys operating in oversight of a general council, the east frequently resented as an act of supremacy it said Jesus never intended. Peter may have been first, the east reasoned, but that did not make him best or supreme. These are some of the reasons why east and west count general councils differently and disagree on which are ecumenical. Ironically, in coming together to solve problems, the first millennium's general councils unintentionally helped divide the church.

BIBLIOGRAPHY

Leo Donald Davis. *The First Seven Ecumenical Councils (325–787): Their History and Theology.* Wilmington, Del.: Michael Glazier, 1987.

W. H. C. Frend. *The Rise of Christianity.* Philadelphia: Fortress Press, 1984.

Peter L'Huillier. *The Church of the Ancient Councils: The Disciplinary Work of the First Four Ecumenical Councils.* Crestwood, N.Y.: St. Vladimir's Seminary Press, 1996.

Part II

COUNCILS IN THE MIDDLE AGES

Overleaf: The Lateran palace and basilica, Rome. Drawing by Marten van Heemskerck, 1535. Courtesy of Kupferstichkabinett, Berlin.

In the Middle Ages, the papacy came into its own, dominating general councils and imposing a largely administrative agenda. This marks a significant change from the councils of the first millennium, when doctrine was the main issue. As we have recounted, the first general councils began under emperors and initially operated outside of papal leadership; only over time did popes like Leo I decisively influence councils. During the Middle Ages, however, papal concerns, particularly with the church's organizational structures and procedures, absorbed the seven general councils held between Lateran I (1123) and Vienne (1311–12).

Most medieval conciliar documents read like papal statements, in which the royal "we" of the pope issues decrees and makes judgments. Where the early church councils asserted, "This holy council declares...," medieval popes frequently called councils to agree with their own binding statements and only sometimes did they add the phrase "with the approval of the sacred council" to the councils' records. These medieval popes at times backed up their authority in these records by referring to the power of the keys given to Peter and his successors. The growth of what has been called "papal monarchy" explains why medieval general councils seem less deliberative than their earlier counterparts.

While theological explanations distinguished the first millennium's councils, legal language marked the medieval meetings. Medieval popes helped develop legal precedent and process in their general councils. During and between general councils, church officials gathered papal statements and judgments into the body, or code, of canon law. A symbiotic relationship developed: A particular pope in council confirmed his predecessors' actions and then added to them at the same council. Later popes might comment on those additions, which another pope in the next council would reassert (though he sometimes changed or revoked them). In this way, the medieval general councils helped construct canon law in stages. Lateran IV (1215) and Lyons I (1245), for instance, gave extensive particulars on legal due process, appeals, and procedures, while Lateran I (1123) legislated against anyone making or passing counterfeit money.

As with the first part, this one looks at each council in turn. These were not the only ecclesial meetings held in the Middle Ages—there were many local councils, some with the pope present—but these seven over the centuries found themselves counted among the twenty-one general councils. The four Lateran councils taken together especially provide evidence of the papal monarchy's growth and attempts to exercise its universal jurisdiction. Popes treated major "international" issues: lay appointment of bishops, heresy, crusades, papal conclaves, and dealing with Jews and Muslims. But at Lyons I and II and Vienne, politics began to dominate; we see the consequences of the papacy's involvement in secular matters. As with Nicaea II, the stories of Lyons I and Vienne prove particularly distressing, for they expose the raw politics and the degree to which the papacy had gotten its nose bloodied. Once again, we will conclude by considering the disciplinary canons that linked the seven medieval general councils together over time.

Chapter 4
Four Lateran Councils:
1123–1215

The first four medieval general councils, Lateran I through IV, met on the pope's home turf in Rome in his own meeting hall. Initially, the Lateran was part of the property Constantine gave to Pope Miltiades in 312 or 313; it was extended into a complex of buildings over the centuries. By holding general councils here, the popes physically backed up their monarchical claim to universal authority in the city of Peter's martyrdom. From this spot, the popes led four councils dealing primarily with church independence, internal legal processes, reform, heretics, other faiths, crusading, and pilgrimage.

Lateran I

Lateran I (1123) was neither a very original council nor one called to meet a pressing theological question. For the most part, Pope Callistus II summoned the council to ratify in a formal, imposing, and universal way recent papal actions taken at regional meetings and in Rome. The major issue for the past fifty years concerned the ongoing question of "investiture," in which laypeople (on the level of emperors, kings, and nobles) appointed bishops or abbots. To grant authority to their chosen officials, these laypeople physically invested them with the symbols of their secular authority (typically a sword or scepter) and their spiritual authority (ring, miter, and crosier).

To an illiterate population, it appeared the bishop or abbot was now the layperson's inferior. Although this may have been the case in terms of property, the papacy could not stand by and let an emperor give the impression that spiritual power was his to give and take away. After decades of battles during which the pope and the emperor fought over their respective rights of appointment, the Concordat of Worms in 1122 settled the issue. According to this compromise, the emperor gave up the right to name church officials or hand them the symbols of their spiritual power; the pope allowed a lay ruler to be present when an official was elected and to give a bishop or abbot the signs of his temporal authority. Lateran I lent authority to the Concordat of Worms by formally approving this settlement at Rome in the pope's presence, beginning the process of papal oversight that marks the four Lateran councils.

Lateran I introduced new items to a general council's agenda: the related issues of pilgrimage and crusading. In 1095, at a local meeting in France, Pope Urban II had called for a crusade to rescue the Holy Land from the Muslims, whom Christians identified as the infidel. About thirty years later, Lateran I pardoned the sins of pilgrims and crusaders as well as protected their families and property while they traveled to Jerusalem. The council nudged those who promised to go on a pilgrimage or crusade but never left home: If they did not fulfill their vow, the council threatened to ban them from churches and, in the case of lay rulers, to withhold most church services and sacraments in their territories. The council also cut off anyone harassing pilgrims to Rome or saints' shrines.

Lateran II

Lateran II (1139), like Lateran I, was neither especially creative nor impressive, but it too contributed to the process whereby the pope gave weight and broad application to decisions made separately in Europe's scattered cities. Half of its canons echoed Lateran I; the other half simply affirmed the decisions of local meetings that had occurred in the sixteen years between Lateran I and II.

Still, Lateran II had several distinguishing characteristics. First, it was somewhat ecumenical: At least one bishop from the east attended, although he was a Latin who held the See of Antioch. Second, it impressed papal unity upon its delegates after a period of schism, a problem that troubled the church throughout the twelfth century, when there were nearly as many antipopes as popes. Pope Honorius II had to deal with a rival, the antipope Celestine II, after a rowdy papal installation featuring an armed assault and physical violence in 1124. When Honorius II died in 1130, a small group of cardinals elected Innocent II in secret while a majority chose Anacletus II, who has come down as an antipope; both men were installed in separate ceremonies on the same day. Anacletus's death in 1138 ended his papal challenges, and the next year Innocent II called Lateran II to help cement his claim to power.

Third, Lateran II dealt with heresy, a central concern for general councils for the next four hundred years. The first millennium's general councils had devoted themselves to the definition of orthodox and heretical doctrines, then established procedures to bring former heretics back into the church. By naming several local instigators as heretics, Lateran II once again made defining and fighting heretics an important piece of business for later general councils, which would spell out in greater detail the rewards due those who opposed the church's challengers.

Lateran III

It is not until Lateran III (1179) that we encounter a general council that can stand alongside the great meetings of the first millennium. Unlike the prior two Lateran councils, Lateran III offered some new legislation and innovative actions. One of the most striking elements was its relatively broad geographic representation—

for a church that would still confine herself to Europe for another three hundred-plus years. Most bishops came from Italy and France, but others arrived from Germany, Spain, Ireland, Scotland, and England. One Hungarian and a Dane stand out, as do seven delegates from the Holy Land, an observer from the Greek churches, and royal envoys.

As with Lateran II, Lateran III asserted papal unity after schism. Three antipopes had already threatened the current pope, Alexander III, and following his council a fourth would as well. Alexander's selection in 1159 had repeated the ugly, confusing elections in 1124 and 1130. To make his leadership and authority clear, Alexander declared null and void all actions taken and every office held by his rivals and their supporters.

More important than this declaration was Lateran III's canon on papal elections, which marked another step in a medieval process that reserved papal elections to the cardinals—even if it meant locking them inside a room. This process had begun in another Lateran synod, one that never reached the list of twenty-one general councils. Pope Nicholas II in 1059 had given the cardinals the leading role in electing the pope in an attempt to counteract the influence of Rome's wealthy families. At the time, however, centuries of precedent also allowed other members of the clergy to participate, let the sitting pope declare his preference for a successor, and imprecisely permitted laypeople (including the emperor) to assent or not.

Alexander III solidified the cardinals' favored position in papal elections with an important canon at Lateran III. Perhaps because his own election was disputed when some participants demanded a unanimous vote, Alexander III restricted a papal election to the cardinals and declared unanimity unnecessary. If a candidate garnered two-thirds of the votes of the cardinals present, he was elected pope. A century later another council, Lyons II in 1274, added the lock-and-key aspect that gave the "conclave" its name ("with a key").

Lateran III continued the fight against heretics, singling out a group called the Cathars ("pure ones") or Albigensians. Cathars rejected most of the Catholic Church's sacramental and belief systems, substituting a minimalist religion based on inner faith and extreme asceticism. Lateran III denied a funeral mass and church burial to a Cathar; it also forbade anyone from giving food and shelter to a Cathar or conducting business with one. The council motivated Christians to fight these heretics when it reduced by two years any penance a defender of the faith may have received. Significantly, this statement granted to those who fought heretics at home the same kind of reward prior councils and popes granted to crusaders battling the "infidel" far away in the Holy Land.

On a similar topic, the council legislated against any Christian helping a Muslim and spelled out particular offenses, apparently as they related to aiding and abetting the crusaders' enemy. Lateran III prohibited Christians from giving arms and wood for helmets, for instance, and from commanding or piloting Muslims' ships. The council showed no mercy to such a traitor: He was excommunicated, lost his property, and could be enslaved. In all other situations, the council declared no Jew or Muslim could hire a Christian servant.

Lateran IV

The increasingly impressive papal meetings culminated in Lateran IV (1215), "the" general council of the Middle Ages. Even more than was the case with Lateran III, the attendance at Lateran IV was large, impressive, and varied. More than four hundred archbishops and bishops, including some from eastern Europe, came with agenda items that Pope Innocent III had asked them to prepare. They joined over eight hundred abbots and priors plus royal ambassadors from Constantinople, England, Germany, Hungary, the Holy Land, France, Aragon, and Portugal. For the first time in the history of general councils, the pope extended participation to heads of religious orders and cathedral chapters. Though invited, no representatives from the Greek churches attended, diminishing Lateran IV's claim to truly ecumenical status. Nevertheless, its documents provide a snapshot of the high medieval church. With its wide attendance, many new canons, and specific concerns, Lateran IV sums up the church's dogma, structure, and problems in the middle of the Middle Ages.

Lateran IV began with a profession of faith, which essentially restated ancient theological principles taken from the first millennium's battles against heresy. It then addressed a standing concern of general councils when it legislated against heretics. This council ordered secular authorities to swear to fight heretics; if leaders failed to get rid of heretics, they might be excommunicated. The council also granted the "crusader indulgence" (remission of sins) to any Christian defending the faith against heretics at home, as Lateran III had already done.

Lateran IV pressed the fight against heresy, excommunicating any Christian who received, defended, or supported heretics. If this Christian did not mend his ways within one year, serious consequences would follow. Such a person could not make a will or inherit; he could not hold public office, vote, or provide testimony. If he were a judge, his sentences would not be enforced nor could he hear any more cases; if he were a notary, his documents would be invalidated; if he were a lawyer, he would be deprived of the right to defend clients. The council especially charged bishops with investigating heresy: If they did not root out heresy, they would be deposed. To prevent heresy from spreading, especially through the many self-appointed preachers wandering around at that time, Lateran IV required all preachers to have a license under the bishop's authority.

Lateran IV called for a new Holy Land crusade to start in 1217 and provided many specific provisions and incentives. Any cleric who went off on crusade would receive his regular pay for three years. The council warned Christians who had promised to leave but had not yet set off to get going. To promote the means of transportation to the Holy Land, the church would remit the sins of those who paid for or built ships. Crusaders would be exempt from taxes and interest payments, but those who helped Muslims would receive punishment, as Lateran III had said. Peace was to reign among Christians for four years, presumably so they could combine and channel their efforts against a common enemy. Finally, the church promised something for nearly everyone: She would pardon the sins of those who went on crusade of their own accord and with their own money, of those who paid to send others but could not go themselves, and of those sent by someone else who paid their way.

This general council also addressed the matter of Christians interacting with Muslims and Jews. Lateran IV required Jews and Muslims to dress distinctly (without providing details) so Christians would know they were dealing with non-Christians. It prohibited Jews from holding public office and so from having authority over Christians. Jews were also confined indoors on Palm Sunday,

> because some of them...do not blush to parade in very ornate dress and are not afraid to mock Christians who are presenting a memorial of the most sacred passion and are displaying signs of grief.

It should be pointed out, however, that Lateran IV tells only half the story: On Palm Sunday and during Holy Week, Jews were often stoned or spat upon, sometimes at the instigation of preachers, and blamed for Jesus' death.

Two other items stand out at Lateran IV. The first concerns the Eucharist. Lateran IV used a relatively new word, "transubstantiation," to describe the ancient doctrine that bread and wine changed into Jesus' body and blood. A later canon demanded the famous "Easter duty," which mandated that every male and female Christian receive the Eucharist at least every Easter as well as confess his or her sins once a year.

Second, Lateran IV anticipated a problem Martin Luther would fight three hundred years later: the sale of indulgences. "The Christian religion is frequently disparaged because certain people put saints' relics up for sale and display them indiscriminately," the council noted. The council said Christians could be deceived by "lying stories or false documents," unintentionally anticipating Chaucer's pardoner, who infamously rattled pigs' bones as phony relics. The council required official control of relics: They must be kept in reliquaries, they could not be sold, and new ones needed papal approval. Lateran IV made every almscollector carry an official letter, effectively his license to practice, and went so far as to provide a model that could be copied easily.

Chapter 5
Power Struggles:
Lyons I (1245) to
Vienne (1311–1312)

Repeating the pattern of the first millennium, the second cluster of general councils during the Middle Ages did not quite live up to the quality of the first. Like their four medieval predecessors, the next three general councils addressed crusading (although the movement was failing), papal conclaves, and heresy, but they were also battered by political entanglements. Most especially, where the Lateran councils demonstrated the papacy's authority, the next three meetings illustrated its limitations in the face of secular force.

Lyons I

Lyons I met in 1245 primarily to depose the emperor, Frederick II, who for a long time had troubled the papacy by trying to take over papal territory and to control the church in the model of Constantine and Charlemagne. The council fathers at Lyons permitted Frederick to send a representative, who pled his case and defended the emperor against charges of interference and heresy. Despite this, Pope Innocent IV declared the emperor excommunicated and deposed; he also released all those under the emperor's authority from their oaths of allegiance, a traditional method used to undercut political, military, and financial support. Innocent recounted his attempts at peace, which he said Frederick had fought, and specifically accused the emperor of inciting people to switch their loyalties from pope to emperor and of disregarding papal authority by "despising the keys of the church."

Ironically, sixteen years before this council Frederick had achieved what many popes supporting the crusades could not: safer access for pilgrims. Lyons II's bull of deposition complained that Frederick had negotiated with Muslims: This charge referred to a successful action the emperor had taken for the good of Christianity. In 1229, while under an earlier church censure, Frederick had negotiated a measure of peace with the sultan of Egypt, who controlled Palestine. This ten-year Treaty of Jaffa gave Christians nominal control of Jerusalem; allowed pilgrims easier access to Bethlehem, Nazareth, and Jerusalem; and permitted Christians and Muslims to practice their faiths side by side. Perhaps Frederick's achievement galled the papacy, as did his other attempts to curtail papal power: invading papal lands and blocking bishops from attending a council in 1241.

On the subject of crusading, Innocent IV closely followed his predecessor Innocent III at Lateran IV, while adding two interesting items that indicate the pressing need for money to finance the military campaigns. First, he declared the rich should curtail extravagant feasting. To promote moderation, the pope promised the wealthy that if they put the money that would have paid for lavish feasts toward the crusading effort, prelates could remit their sins. Second, he hoped the dying would leave some money to help the crusades. Innocent IV directed prelates and their clergy to

> persuade the faithful committed to your care, in your sermons or when you impose a penance upon them, granting a special indulgence, as you see it to be expedient, that in their wills, in return for the remission of their sins, they should leave something for the help of the holy land or the eastern empire.

With regard to other matters that had concerned the four Lateran councils, Lyons I did not promulgate any canons concerning reform or heresy, but it did address many details on legal procedures, judgments, and appeals. There was so much politics, so little participation, and such a small attendance (about 150 delegates at most), however, that Lyons I falls into line as a close second behind Constantinople IV as the least impressive general council. Like Constantinople IV, it took centuries for Lyons I even to make the list of the church's twenty-one general councils.

Lyons II

Lyons II under Gregory X in 1274 is more impressive, but it also indicates the papacy's evaporating dominance, at least in contrast to Innocent III at Lateran IV. As with Lateran IV, the pope called for and received preparatory reports and suggestions from bishops in the field. Several items led the agenda but two, reform and crusading, bore little fruit. Lyons II is notable mostly for its additional rules on papal elections and its fragile—and ultimately temporary—unification of the western and eastern churches.

Unlike most of its immediate predecessors, Lyons II was truly ecumenical. The eastern emperor, Michael VIII Palaeologus, reached out to Gregory X because he needed western support to stave off invasions of his territories from several fronts. Though the council started without them, when the eastern bishops arrived everyone took up the issues surrounding unification, especially papal primacy and the doctrine represented by the Latin word *filioque*.

The word *filioque* is part of the doctrinal statement that the Holy Spirit proceeds from the Father *and the Son*. The issue for the east concerned not so much the doctrinal assertion itself as the way the west had introduced it. This word does not appear in the creed of Constantinople I but was later added in Latin, western translations. Over time, the word was alternately included and omitted in the west; most conspicuous is the example of Pope Leo III (795–816) posting a creed without *filioque* in Rome. But by about 1000, the west accepted the doctrine and the word as normative.

Easterners objected to this addition because it did not have an ecumenical council's approval. At Chalcedon, as we have already noted, the fathers declared no one could think, teach, or write down doctrinal statements other than those contained in the creeds of Nicaea I, Constantinople I, and Chalcedon; in Cyril of Alexandria's second letter to Nestorius and his letter on peace to John of Antioch; and in Leo I's *Tome*. In the opinion of most in the east, unilaterally slipping in this supplementary word *filioque* violated this principle. Specifically, it provided an example of the papal supremacy the east was not willing to ascribe to Rome, even as it recognized Rome had a certain primacy because of Peter.

From early in the church's history and continuing through the Middle Ages, many eastern churches accepted Rome's primacy among the five patriarchates of Rome, Constantinople, Antioch, Alexandria, and Jerusalem. But at the same time they contended the government of the church rested among the five together, ideally at an ecumenical council. By extension, they argued the Roman bishop did not have universal jurisdiction, could not interfere in the affairs of another patriarchal see, and certainly could not make changes binding on other bishops—let alone on his own. For easterners, the insertion of *filioque*, like the manner in which Leo I took it upon himself to strike down Chalcedon's canon 28 placing Constantinople second in line after Rome, represented just such an abuse of authority.

Surprisingly, the eastern delegates did not ultimately protest either papal primacy or *filioque* at Lyons II, which in its first canon declared:

> ...[T]he holy spirit proceeds eternally from the father and the son, not as from two principles, but as from one principle....[T]his is the unchangeable and true belief of the orthodox fathers and doctors, Latin and Greek alike.

The emperor asked if the east could keep its own creed and Gregory complied. The agreement did not stand up over time back in the east, however, and very quickly east and west again split; this situation would repeat itself in 1439 during one phase of the general council of Basel-Ferrara-Florence-Rome, which revisited many of these key issues.

Lyons II is also noteworthy for officially giving the church her papal conclaves. Like Alexander III, who had previously legislated on papal elections at Lateran III, Gregory X was elected in a raucous scene. Cardinals had met intermittently over the course of almost three years in Viterbo; city officials grew so tired of waiting they locked the cardinals in a building. When they still could not decide, the officials ripped off the roof and said they would supply only bread and water if the cardinals did not elect a pope immediately, which they did.

As a consequence of this and other irregularities over the centuries, Gregory X with his council affirmed Lateran III's rules and laid down additional procedures that have stood since then with few modifications. The goals were quick elections and short papal vacancies. The cardinals must gather in the city where the pope died within ten days of his death. (Today, no matter where the pope dies, the conclave will open in Rome fifteen to twenty days later.) They are to be completely secluded and physically locked away "with a key": *cum clave,* hence *conclave.* To speed things up, the cardinals would not receive any of the money due them from the papal treasury while they met. Should three days go by without an election, food would be restricted to only one dish twice a day; after five more days, the cardinals would get only bread, water, and wine.

Vienne

By the time of the next council, Vienne in 1311–12, the papacy had slipped further under secular influence. Vienne met near the beginning of the papacy's long stay in Avignon where, to varying degrees, the French crown influenced the popes. This council represents the high—or low—point of that influence: The French king Philip IV (the Fair) bullied Pope Clement V into giving in to him, largely by continually threatening to put a prior pope, Boniface VIII, on trial for heresy.

Philip had fiercely fought Boniface's efforts to bring the church in France under his power. During their drawn-out battles, Philip had cut off the flow of money to Rome from France and intimidated many French bishops. In response, Boniface repeatedly scolded the king and declared that his papal authority overruled kings and emperors. As Boniface prepared to excommunicate the French king in 1303, Philip's military force assaulted the pope, who died shortly afterward.

Philip found Clement V a pliable pope and instigated the Council of Vienne, which was burdened with political intrigue from the start. Clement originally summoned some, not all, of the church's bishops; Philip reviewed the list and struck more names off. Fewer than two hundred eventually attended this council, which met only rarely in general assembly and never for discussion. In full session, the delegates simply approved what committees and the pope together with his cardinals had already decided—and even then always under the shadow of Philip's threat to put Boniface on trial as a heretic if things did not go the king's way.

Philip's central concern was getting rid of the Knights of the Temple. The Templars, as they were known, were monk-knights established about two hundred years earlier under a rule written by Bernard of Clairvaux; they dedicated themselves to protecting the Holy Land and its pilgrims. Aside from a standing army in Palestine, the Templars held much property in Europe, and its income supported their military actions overseas. Since 1291, when the Muslims conquered the last strong European presence in the Holy Land and wiped out many Templars, the order had fallen on hard times and no longer fulfilled its mandate. Templars did, however, continue to operate as bankers and property managers, often in luxurious settings in Europe. These factors made them an inviting target for Philip, who was deep in debt.

Playing on their recent setbacks, in the years before and during Vienne, Philip engineered a French investigation into the Templars' supposedly shady business affairs and allegedly heretical, immoral actions. A number of knights confessed to an initiation rite that included denying Jesus and spitting on a cross; they were also charged with idolatry and scandalous sexual practices. But Vienne's records do not reflect all the facts. Investigations in other countries largely exonerated the order; knights who confessed later retracted their statements, saying they had been coerced by torture. According to the official documents, however, the council rigidly followed due process and neither used physical force nor made threats to those under investigation, and knights who confessed stood by their statements.

Philip won with respect to the Templars at Vienne, but not entirely. Clement V dissolved the order and a number of knights, including the grand master, were subsequently burned at the stake. Simply put, Clement V was too weak to resist what history records as a railroading of the order. However, though the pope ordered the Templars out of existence, he did not pronounce them guilty or innocent of heresy. In addition, Clement did not give their money and property to Philip, as the king clearly desired, but granted the Templars' material goods to another order, the Hospitallers, and established rules for their oversight. For several years, Philip managed to have some control over the property and directed funds into his own treasury.

Perhaps the most disturbing element of the story of the Templars at Vienne is Clement's description of Philip. Clement did not put Boniface on trial for heresy, as the king hoped, but amazingly the current pope singled out his predecessor's enemy for praise. Clement mentioned "our dear son in Christ, Philip, the illustrious king of France" and praised his zeal for the church, adding: "He was not moved by greed. He had no intention of claiming or appropriating for himself anything from the Templars' property."

Though not the only business conducted at Vienne, the affair of the Templars was the most notorious. The council also addressed heresy among other groups and set up procedures for inquisition and punishment. These steps indicate that heresy continued to be a problem for the church in spite of the Lateran councils' rules for investigating dissent.

Vienne specifically outlawed two groups, the Beguines and the Beghards, especially in Germany. These were free-floating crowds of believers, many of them women, who did not fit into established groups of faithful Christians. They seemed more dedicated to religious practices than other laypeople, yet they were not vowed or professed members of existing religious orders of monks, friars, or nuns and did not wish to be. A number of Beguines and Beghards did resist some of the church's sacraments and hierarchical structures, but Vienne's canons portrayed these movements as much more organized and systematic than they actually were, which may have made it easier to condemn them en masse.

As Lateran IV had done, Vienne specifically told bishops to find and fight heretics in their dioceses. The council warned against inquisitorial excesses, but ordered bishops to investigate charges with vigor, diligence, and fairness.

> If they fail, because of hatred, favor, affection, money or temporal advantage, to proceed against someone when they ought, against justice and their conscience, then the bishop or superior is suspended from office for three years....

One last item stands out. Vienne's proceedings include a canon calling for improved education in languages for the purpose of evangelization among non-Christians. The pope ordered scholars appointed wherever the roving Roman curia was located and at each of the major university centers: Paris, Oxford, Bologna, and Salamanca. Specifically, he wanted to see learning and fluency in Hebrew, Arabic, and Chaldaic (which probably referred to all other Semitic languages, including Aramaic). This was no offhand wish: Clement wanted two professors of each language in each location to translate works from these languages into Latin. At a council known for its capitulation to royal power and a generally timid papal stance, this canon highlights the renewed interest in biblical literature among humanists and professors that would revitalize scripture study over the next several centuries.

Chapter 6
Supervising the
Medieval Church:
Disciplinary Canons

The seven medieval general councils, like those of the first millennium, addressed the organization and administration of the church as an institution. These disciplinary canons were in addition to the specific business each of the medieval meetings conducted along with their shared, intermittent attention to crusading, heresy, Jews and Muslims, and papal conclaves. The canons dealt primarily with clerical education and behavior, bishops and church freedom, and—new for general councils—usury, marriage, and societal violence.

A familiar pattern reemerged: Councils repeated themselves, indicating some Christians kept disobeying earlier regulations. Canons had to be reiterated to make sure clergy and laity followed the rules. Moreover, to show how their canons tied into a longer history, medieval councils sometimes noted they were reaffirming requirements from prior general councils, especially those held during the first millennium.

Clergy

Medieval councils wanted to make sure the church ordained bishops and priests who were properly educated and morally worthy to serve and who avoided material attachments. Lateran III spelled out the minimum requirements for a bishop: He must be at least thirty years old, of legitimate birth, and "worthy by his life and learning." Priests should be at least twenty-five and win approval of their behavior and knowledge. A later canon from Lateran III was more specific and reminds us of rules laid down by Chalcedon, Nicaea II, and Constantinople IV prohibiting clergy from managing property because this duty stained them with worldliness. A cleric could not involve himself in secular legal cases "on the grounds that, neglecting his duty as a cleric, he plunges into the waves of this world to please its princes."

Church officials knew some bishops did not enforce Lateran III's rules. A century later, Lyons II noted that many ignored the earlier stipulation that parish priests be twenty-five with approved education and morality.

> Since many neglect to observe this canon, we wish their dangerous negligence to be made good by observance of the law. We therefore decree that nobody is to be appointed parish priest unless he is suitable by knowledge, morals, and age. Any appointments from now of those younger than 25 are to lack all validity. The person appointed is obliged to reside in the parish church of which he has become rector, in order that he may take more diligent care of the flock entrusted to him.

Vienne encouraged clerics to persevere in a holy life but complained they rushed through their prayers, left parts out, and gossiped as they prayed. Some arrived late for services and departed early, even bringing their hunting dogs and birds with them to church.

To improve a priest's training and subsequent service, Lateran III and IV legislated regulations for clerical education. Lateran III required money to be set aside in each cathedral for a professor to teach clergy and the poor. Lateran IV, after repeating word for word Lateran III's canon on education, observed: "This decree, however, is very little observed in many churches." Lateran IV expanded its predecessor's canon by stipulating that each cathedral, plus other churches that could afford it, must allocate a salary for a professor who would teach grammar. In addition, the largest churches must add a second professor for practical theology and scripture. Lateran IV three times ordered bishops to instruct and ordain only qualified candidates, "for it is preferable, especially in the ordination of priests, to have a few good ministers than many bad ones."

Worldliness

Again and again, medieval councils had to treat clerical behavior, which did not seem to have improved much despite the complaints the first millennium's councils had made. Once more, councils targeted the unholy trinity of simony, pluralism, and absenteeism, particularly because these transgressions prevented priests from exercising their pastoral duties. Lateran I, II, and III repeatedly mourned and condemned these problems. Lateran IV cited Lateran III's rule against pluralism but admitted "none or little fruit is resulting from this statute."

The four Lateran councils renewed the attack on concubinage and clerical marriage. Lateran II stepped up the assault by telling laypeople to avoid mass offered by a priest who lived with a woman, by demanding this man and woman separate, and by declaring they were not truly married. (The next canon applied this nonmarriage clause equally to nuns who took husbands.) Lateran II then addressed a consequent predicament: Married priests sometimes passed their parishes down to their sons like a family business. To avoid this problem, Lateran II forbade hereditary rights to church buildings and jobs; if a priest's son wanted to serve at the altar, he had to be attached to a monastery.

Councils also wanted to make sure priests looked and acted their part. Vienne explained the clergy's "outward garb should reveal their inner integrity." Lateran II told priests to comport themselves properly, to look and act holy, and to avoid excess in their clothing. Lateran IV was more specific. Outer garments must be closed and not very short or long; clothes should not be red or green or have long sleeves; shoes could not have embroidery or pointed toes; no decorations should adorn bridles, saddles, spurs, buckles, and belts. Vienne threatened a cleric with loss of his revenues for up to a year if he wore striped clothes or checkered, red, or green boots in public. It also prohibited "a gown or tabard [sleeveless tunic] which is furred to the edge and so short that the lower garment is clearly seen."

Councils frequently regulated the clergy's behavior in and out of church. Lateran II barred clerics from practicing medicine or civil law. Lateran IV prohibited the clergy from any actions that shed blood: surgery, duels, combat, blessing ordeals, ordering physical punishment or being present during its administration. Clergy should not take part in drinking games or hunting and must avoid theaters, taverns, and gambling. Vienne added to this list butchering, running an inn, engaging in any secular business or trade, and carrying arms.

Monks, Nuns, Friars

Councils paid special attention to monks, nuns, and friars during the medieval explosion in religious orders. Lateran I and IV reiterated the bishops' oversight of monks: Lateran I required them to live in cloister, and Lateran IV reminded religious orders to appoint supervisors to visit male and female monasteries, to inquire what was happening, and to order changes if necessary. The monks themselves were to gather for a general meeting in every province or kingdom once every three years. Lateran II said monks and nuns should not sing their daily prayers together.

Vienne devoted a long canon to monks, requiring of them modesty in dress and lifestyle in words very similar to Lateran IV's and Vienne's rules for priests. Monks must confess their sins and receive the Eucharist at least once a month. The canon required one monk to explain aspects of his order's rule in the vernacular to other monks; if possible, a professor should be paid for basic and advanced education. Vienne's next canon targeted problems in convents and required the bishop to visit each one every year.

> The visitors are to be very careful that the nuns—some of whom, to our sorrow, we have heard are transgressors—do not wear silk, various furs or sandals; do not wear their hair long in a horn-shaped style, nor make use of striped and multi-colored caps; do not attend dances and the banquets of seculars; do not go walking through the streets and towns by day or night; and do not lead a luxurious life in other ways.

Lateran IV had forbidden new orders and told people to join existing ones that had already been approved. Lyons II repeated this rule but recognized that it was being ignored by many unaffiliated groups operating on their own authority. This council gave special treatment to the Franciscans and Dominicans, even though they gained official church status after Lateran IV's prohibition in 1215, since "their approval bears witness to their evident advantage to the universal church."

Because of persistent tension between diocesan priests and mendicant friars during the Middle Ages, however, the council ordered friars to operate within certain parameters. Friars were permitted to preach in their own churches but not in parish churches unless the parish priests invited them; friars could not preach anything against the bishop or try to woo the congregation to a mendicant parish. Friars also had to seek permission from the parish priest to administer extreme unction, say mass, or witness marriages in his church; the bishop must give mendicants specific permission to hear confessions in his territory.

Bishops

Bishops did not escape the councils' calls for reform. Lateran IV scolded church officials about late-night parties and gossip ("not to mention other things") that made them bleary-eyed the next morning. Some celebrated mass only four times a year; others did not even attend. Lateran III and IV complained that prelates overused and misused the penalty of excommunication. Lateran III reminded them they must not accept money for sacraments or promise to fill a vacant office before the current occupant left or died. Lyons II repeated a prior rule against making a payoff to avoid a bishop's visitation. To give the ban teeth, the council demanded the offending person pay back double the bribe he had taken.

Vienne continued the councils' assault against episcopal abuse, surely because the bishop should promote positive change and promote an exemplary model for clerics and laypeople. Vienne criticized prelates who demanded extravagance and money during (or in lieu of) their visitations to monasteries and who treated religious orders harshly by destroying their property, ignoring their rights, and placing their relatives in the order. This same council, on the other hand, twice offered support to bishops against their enemies.

Church Freedom

The councils also attempted to protect the church's freedom in their disciplinary decrees. One issue concerned appointments to high church office and the investiture ceremony that symbolized them. Lateran I affirmed the bishop's right to appoint officials below him in his own diocese. Lateran II and III also denied laypeople and religious orders the right to make and receive such appointments or generally to disregard the bishop's authority. Lateran IV declared elections made "through abuse of the secular power" invalid and removed the person appointed from his office. All four Lateran councils and Lyons II legislated against a related problem: lay control of church property and funds. Lateran IV described the matter very directly when it declared, "Lay people, however devout, have no power to dispose of church property."

Laypeople

Although medieval general councils focused to a great degree on clerical conduct and church business, several of their measures touched laypeople below the aristocracy. One item was usury, the process by which a moneylender charged interest, often exorbitant, on a loan. Christians could not make money on money. Lateran III forbade Christians from practicing usury and added a stiff penalty: "Notorious usurers" could not receive communion or a Christian burial. Lyons II backed Lateran III in sharp language:

> Wishing to close up the abyss of usury, which devours souls and swallows up property, we order under threat of the divine malediction that the constitution of the Lateran council against usurers be inviolably observed....[T]he less convenient it is for usurers to lend, the more their freedom to practice usury is curtailed.

To make things less convenient for usurers, Lyons II forbade renting houses to them. Lyons II denied Christian usurers a church burial, declared their wills invalid, and told clerics they could not hear their confessions or absolve them unless restitution was made or provided for. Vienne said bishops and inquisitors should pursue and punish as a heretic anyone who denied that usury was sinful.

The medieval church's rule against Christians lending money with interest frequently created a formula for trouble. Since a number of trades were closed to Jews, they had to do their best within the businesses open to them in order to survive economically. Jews could charge interest, so Christians who needed money banked with them. In language offensive to modern ears, Lateran IV portrayed the situation the church had, in part, forced onto Jews.

> The more the Christian religion is restrained from usurious practices, so much the more does the perfidy of the Jews grow in these matters, so that within a short time they are exhausting the resources of Christians. Wishing therefore to see that Christians are not savagely oppressed by Jews in this matter, we ordain by this synodal decree that if Jews in future, on any pretext, extort oppressive and excessive interest from Christians, then they are to be removed from contact with Christians until they have made adequate satisfaction for the immoderate burden. Christians too, if need be, shall be compelled by ecclesiastical censure, without the possibility of an appeal, to abstain from commerce with them.

Financial exchange between Christians and Jews bound by these principles naturally led to conflicts and contributed to the kind of anti-Semitism that would be portrayed several centuries later in Shakespeare's *The Merchant of Venice,* especially through the character Shylock.

Marriage

Another area directly touching the laity dealt with marriage and consanguinity. If two people who were related by blood wanted to get married, how close a relation was too close? Lateran I and II called marriage among relatives incestuous. These councils said both divine and secular law prohibited the practice. They also noted that secular laws prevented a person guilty of marrying a relative from claiming an inheritance. But neither council defined just how close a link of blood constituted the permitted or prohibited "degree" of consanguinity.

By not specifying degrees of relation, the church left herself open to a problem. Medieval society was not very mobile: Most people in the Middle Ages never traveled more than a good walking distance from their homes. A huge percentage of Europe's population lived and died in the same location, a relatively isolated piece of the countryside. Since most medieval people spent their entire lives in a closed world, sooner or later the pool of eligible partners would disappear if villagers related to one another even remotely could not marry. If they could not, communities (and the church herself) would quickly die out because Christian adults could not produce Christian babies.

At Lateran IV, the pope recognized the difficulties and cut down the restrictions. In an interesting example of papal authority, Innocent III revoked the canons from the general councils Lateran I and II, though he was careful to say he did so "with the approval of this sacred council [Lateran IV]." Now, no one could marry within just four degrees of consanguinity, which generally translated into a prohibition against marrying anyone closer than a second cousin.

Stopping Violence

The first three Lateran councils repeatedly issued restrictions against the violence plaguing Europe's most vulnerable people. We can group the first canons under what is called the Peace or Truce of God. These were directives issued by church leaders and designed to curtail the roving bands of mercenaries that occasionally ransacked the European landscape, threatening families and the farms on which they relied for food and income. An example is the declaration that fighting could only take place on Mondays, Tuesdays, and Wednesdays throughout the year, but not at all during the Advent-Christmas-Epiphany and Lent-Easter-Pentecost seasons.

A second group of canons specifically deplored violence taken against innocent Christians. Lateran II said all priests, clerics, monks, pilgrims, merchants, and peasants, together with their livestock, should be allowed to travel and work unmolested. (Clerics and pilgrims could not carry arms even for their own defense, though the latter often stuck metal points onto the end of their wooden walking staffs.) Excommunication was the penalty for anyone who attacked a cleric or monk, or who violated the principle of sanctuary by laying hands on a person who sought refuge in a church or cemetery.

Two other types of canons against violence stand out. One batch of canons targeted jousts and tournaments, presumably because they diverted money, material, and men from the crusades. To promote compliance, the councils ruled that if a knight died during one of these festivals, he lost his right to a church burial. Another canon, this one from Lateran II, singled out arsonists with very imposing words:

> We completely detest and forbid, by the authority of God and the blessed apostles Peter and Paul, that most dreadful, devastating, and malicious crime of incendiarism. For this pernicious and inimical calamity surpasses all other kinds of destruction.

73

Arsonists risked excommunication and the loss of church burial. Repentant arsonists were ordered to pay for their damage, then spend a year in pilgrimage and service to the Holy Land or Spain. When it came to preventing violence, the medieval general councils meant business.

BIBLIOGRAPHY

Joseph H. Lynch. *The Medieval Church: A Brief History.* London: Longman, 1992.

Colin Morris. *The Papal Monarchy: The Western Church from 1050 to 1250.* Oxford: Clarendon Press, 1989.

Paul B. Pixton. *The German Episcopacy and the Implementation of the Decrees of the Fourth Lateran Council, 1216–1245: Watchmen on the Tower.* Leiden: E. J. Brill, 1995.

Part III

COUNCILS IN THE ERA OF REFORMATIONS

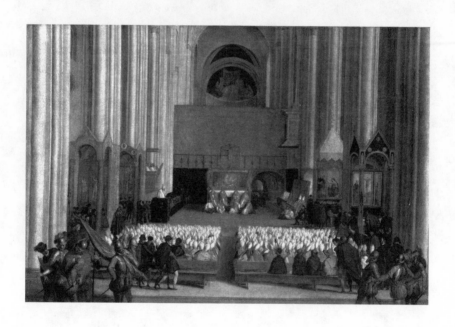

Overleaf: The Council of Trent, anonymous sixteenth-century artist, from the Louvre, Paris. Courtesy of Giraudon/Art Resource, N.Y.

The history of the church's general councils takes several interesting turns in the later Middle Ages, and then a few more in the sixteenth century around the time of the Protestant and Catholic disputes. Struggles about the relative authority of popes and general councils nearly overwhelmed the fifteenth-century councils: Constance (1414–18) and Basel-Ferrara-Florence-Rome (1431–45). The next two general councils, Lateran V (1512–17) and Trent (ca. 1545–63), cannot be separated from the unprecedented context of growing demands for reform. The hierarchy's persistent resistance to effective reforms, which were desperately needed, led to the challenges launched against the Roman Catholic Church by Martin Luther, Jean Calvin, and others. These challenges were what the great reform council of Trent responded to, in large part. In the history of the general councils, these four stand apart in their own unique chapter.

Chapter 7
Councils vs. Popes:
Constance (1414–1418)
and Basel-Ferrara-
Florence-Rome
(1431–1445)

It is impossible to understand Constance and Basel-Ferrara-Florence-Rome apart from the Great Western Schism (1378–1417). Just as important was the challenge of a wide-ranging idea called conciliarism, which to various degrees held that a general council was more powerful than a pope—or at least held authority equal to the papacy's. "What is a general council's power and position?" became the key question in the fifteenth century. For that reason, we must explore its background at some length before examining Constance and Basel-Ferrara-Florence-Rome.

Great Western Schism and Conciliarism

The Great Western Schism does not refer to the split between the eastern (Greek) and western (Latin) churches, but to a period of almost forty years in the western church when two, and then three, popes claimed to be the true successor to Peter and the real bishop of Rome. The situation began in 1378 when a divided group of cardinals meeting to elect a new pope compromised on a candidate outside the conclave. He took the name Urban VI and is known, along with his successors, as the "Roman" pope. Soon after, Urban VI began browbeating the cardinals to such a degree that they claimed his election had been invalid on the grounds that they had voted in fear of a mob rioting outside the conclave. These cardinals defected and held a new election later in 1378. The pope they chose, Clement VII, and his successor, Benedict XIII, are known as the "Avignon" popes because they lived mostly in southern France, where the papacy had resided for much of the fourteenth century. The Roman and Avignon popes excommunicated each other and appointed their own sets of cardinals, so not only were there two popes, but there were two competing papacies with two curias and two colleges of cardinals. Europe divided as countries lined up behind one or the other pope.

About the same time the schism occurred, a discussion about conciliar authority, which had been bubbling throughout the fourteenth century, became more relevant, especially as the fifteenth century began and the schism continued. Conciliarism was not one solid, undisputed concept. It had many roots and branches, some of which can be seen as more or less "constitutional" or "democratic." Most conciliarists held some form of this main idea: The church was a corporate body. Although the church had a head—the pope who is the vicar of Christ—the church was not supposed to be a monarchy. All of the different versions of conciliarism shared the idea that all those affected by a certain law or action had a right to give their opinion, sometimes in their own voices but more practically through representatives.

The most radical conciliarists believed the highest authority in the church was ultimately a general council, regardless of whether the pope attended or not. Other conciliarists saw a kind of partnership between pope and council but tended to give the papacy only the status of a delegated or administrative authority. The pope would be like a prime minister whom the council appointed; when the council delegated authority to the pope, it did not abdicate its own sovereignty but retained power. Since it gave a pope power, the council remained greater than the pope and it could withdraw that power—something like impeaching a president or voting "no confidence" on a prime minister to force resignation.

A middle-of-the-road version of conciliarism came from the college of cardinals. Many cardinals believed they were an indispensable part of the body of the papacy, like a noble aristocracy or the Roman senate, who shared in the pope's authority. They drew strength for their position from the facts that they voted for the pope in conclave and received part of the papal revenues. Some cardinals believed they, acting as the church's most esteemed representatives, could lead a movement against a bad pope.

Conciliarism did not come from nowhere: A number of church traditions supported some conciliar ideas. One precedent for the conciliarist position reflected the relationship between an abbot and his monks. Monastic tradition had long held that when an abbot or abbess was to be elected or when important decisions had to be made for the monastery, the monks or nuns gathered together to vote, because all had a stake in the outcome. Sometimes, a delegation of older, wiser monks or nuns could decide for the entire community; this procedure became important for the cardinals, who regarded themselves as the older, wiser members of the church's body. Another precedent occurred at medieval universities where individual students and faculty members could vote on certain issues. Sometimes, they gathered together by nationality or academic discipline to cast a bloc vote. Some conciliarists found more ancient precedents supporting their position in the first communities described in the Acts of the Apostles, in the "Council of Jerusalem," and in the earliest general councils (especially Nicaea I, Constantinople I, and to some extent Ephesus) because the pope's role at them was relatively minor, if not nonexistent.

On the other side of the debate about conciliar and papal authority, papalists said only a pope could call a general council: Without a pope, there was in fact no legitimate general council, despite what its members might say about their own gathering. Moreover, according to this position, a pope could go his entire papacy without calling a general council; if he did call one, he was clearly in charge and he had to ratify the council's decisions in order for them to take effect. The papalists, however, had a hard time making their case because the papacy itself—one or the other or both, depending on where you stood during the schism—was creating the need for a resolution.

The Rome-Avignon split gave conciliarists the chance to put their ideas into practice. The extreme and extraordinary circumstance of the Great Western Schism seemed to fit their case exactly. It appeared a general council could, and now would, take place without a pope.

Frustrated cardinals from both the Roman and Avignon curias came together to call a council at Pisa in 1409. Though we have not dwelt on councils like Pisa that did not make the "top twenty-one" list of general councils, this meeting eventually led to the conciliar resolution of the schism at Constance. The cardinals believed they had the authority to call Pisa because the schism was an emergency situation; as part of the papacy and as the church's wiser segment, they had a duty to protect the church. The cardinals met over the objections of the Roman and Avignon popes, neither of whom accepted the council at Pisa.

The Pisan council deposed the Avignon pope Benedict XIII and the Roman pope Gregory XII on the charges of heresy and schism. The problem at Pisa was that not everyone agreed on the solution to the schism. In their rush to elect a pope who would theoretically gain everyone's obedience, the cardinals did not make sure everybody involved would follow the new pope, whoever he was. Without this prior agreement to accept whoever was elected, the schism of two papacies split further into three papacies. The "conciliar" or "Pisan" pope, Alexander V, could not rally all Christians around him and gain complete acceptance, even though the cardinals at Pisa elected him unanimously. Alexander V then named his own college of cardinals, bringing the total to three popes, three curias, and three colleges of cardinals. Pisa only made matters worse.

Constance

It fell to another general council a few years later, Constance (1414–18), to achieve union, but this general council had to operate under the constant, menacing shadow Pisa had cast. If Constance could not resolve the schism, now even more difficult because of three papacies instead of just two, the church faced a division that could remain permanently. The very idea of a general council was also at stake; past councils had helped resolve problems, but Pisa had created a worse situation than it had received. Fortunately, the meeting at Constance brought together Christianity's finest minds in a general council that was arguably the most impressive in history. Nearly three dozen cardinals of all three obediences joined hundreds of archbishops, bishops, and abbots as well as several hundred theologians and canon lawyers. The feeling was that if this meeting could not resolve the schism, nothing could. The church stood on one of the most dangerous brinks in her life.

Constance had one advantage over Pisa from the start: One of the contending popes had called it, giving the meeting some legitimacy. After Alexander V died, John XXIII succeeded him as the Pisan/conciliar pope. (His name and number—John XXIII—is correct. As we will see, he was deposed in 1415, freeing up the name to be selected again by Angelo Roncalli when he was elected pope in 1958.) John XXIII called the council at Constance under pressure, because like the other two popes he feared deposition. But the Holy Roman Emperor-elect at the time, Sigismund, seemed to favor John XXIII, and so this pope counted on being reelected even if Constance deposed him. With Sigismund's protection, John XXIII apparently believed he could control Constance. The Avignon pope, Benedict XIII, never recognized Constance and did not participate in any way; the Roman pope, Gregory XII, sent a pair of delegates to represent him.

The general council at Constance laid down three major tasks for itself: uniting the church under one pope, reforming the church, and dealing with heresy. The matter of unification took precedence, but within the context of major questions about papal and conciliar authority. John XXIII sparked a crisis when it became clear the general council might not automatically reelect him after he agreed to abdicate. Calculating that the council's validity would be called into doubt if the pope who convened the meeting deserted it, John XXIII fled Constance in the middle of the night on 20/21 March 1415. The reaction, after the initial confusion, was not what John XXIII had expected.

Relying on decades of conciliar developments, the members of the general council of Constance asserted themselves by saying they were meeting under their own authority and did not need a pope to continue their deliberations. Jean Gerson, a University of Paris theologian and moderate conciliarist, electrified the council by preaching a sermon on John 12:35, which began with the engaging words, "Walk while you have the light, so that the darkness may not overtake you." Gerson gave his sermon just two days after John XXIII disappeared. His words not only calmed the council but pointed members in their next direction by carefully justifying their actions.

Gerson provided a theology of the general council based on the Holy Spirit. He distilled several key conciliar ideas. The council was assembled legally and could validate itself by the grace of the Holy Spirit. The general council truly represents the church; all Christians, including the pope, were bound to obey it. More specifically related to the schism, Gerson said the general council at Constance could "divorce" the pope. He also claimed a council could meet without papal approval in certain circumstances and that the current one, with several people saying they were the true pope, was just the sort of situation where a general council should step in.

Within two weeks of Gerson's sermon, the Constance delegates codified important parts of Gerson's ideas in the decree *Haec*

86

sancta synodus ("This holy synod"), which repeated some of Gerson's most essential points nearly word for word.

> This holy synod of Constance...legitimately assembled in the holy spirit...has power immediately from Christ;...[E]veryone of whatever state or dignity, even papal, is bound to obey it in those matters which pertain to the faith, the eradication of the said schism, and the general reform of the said church of God in head and members.

After *Haec sancta synodus*, Constance moved quickly to exercise the ultimate authority it claimed in this statement.

The first action was to depose John XXIII in May 1415. Then, in large part to demonstrate the council's competence and authority to judge a matter of faith, the delegates took up the charges of heresy against a popular Czech reformer, priest, and preacher named Jan Hus. The case against Hus has been the subject of much debate, then and now. In 1999, for instance, Pope John Paul II expressed "deep regret for the cruel death inflicted on Jan Hus." The controversy arose because Hus was caught in a power struggle: The council seemed more interested in demonstrating it could sit in judgment than in fully and fairly investigating just what theological and reform positions Hus held, some of which were very justifiable criticisms of the church's worldliness.

Hus was also double-crossed: Although Sigismund had promised Hus he could come to Constance, explain himself, and leave safely, shortly after Hus showed up he was thrown into prison. Hus did not completely help his own cause. In defending himself, he was somewhat noncommittal in responding to certain questions, even while denying some charges against him. The council condemned Hus when he refused to recant certain positions (probably because he did not hold them—or at least did not hold them in the way the council proposed) and because he questioned the council's authority to decide on matters of faith. Declared a heretic and defrocked, Hus was burned at the stake on 6 July 1415.

At the time these events took place, members of the council worked to resolve the schism. Gregory XII, the Roman pope, agreed to resign for the good of the church, but not before his two delegates formally convoked the council in his name. This move gave legitimacy, in Gregory XII's eyes, to any further actions Constance would take while also improving the standing of the Roman claim to the See of Peter and to its continuity of succession. With John XXIII and Gregory XII out of the way, the delegates and Sigismund himself maneuvered to force Benedict XIII to resign, which he never did. Fearing additional schism, Constance proceeded very slowly. It did not want to be accused of rushing to elect and making a bad situation worse, which is precisely what had happened at Pisa in 1409. Only when the members could prove they had exhausted every effort did they finally depose Benedict XIII in July 1417.

Because of the ever present shadow of Pisa, between 1415 and 1417 Constance had progressed cautiously on the issue of how to elect the new pope when that time came. In March 1415, the council said no new cardinals should be created because this would only add to the confusion of loyalties. A few months later, the members declared they must approve the manner in which the next pope would be chosen and prohibited any of the three current claimants from being elected (or reelected, depending on one's perspective). Two years later, in the summer of 1417, they made it a point to say they had moved slowly, carefully, and legally so far. Then they decided, "for this time only," given the extraordinary circumstances, to amend the papal election rules of two earlier general councils, Lateran III and Lyons II.

The delegates at Constance thought it best to create a broader conclave. They feared the competing colleges of cardinals would split in different directions and create an endless conclave where no one candidate could claim the necessary percentage of votes. They decided that, in addition to the twenty-three cardinals, six delegates would represent each of five "nations" or groups of countries (Italy; France; Spain; England, which included Scotland and Ireland; and Germany, which also encompassed Scandinavia and eastern Europe). The winning candidate needed not only two-thirds of the cardinals' votes, but two-thirds of each of the five nations' votes, too. The goal was a clear consensus that would prevent another Pisa.

Remarkably, after thirty-nine years of schism, this expanded conclave in November 1417 took only three days to elect as pope a cardinal named Odo Colonna, who at various times had backed Gregory XII, the Pisan council, and John XXIII. He took the name Martin V, and his papacy successfully held all of Europe's allegiance. The schism was over—and a general council had ended it.

Throughout all of these events, Constance tried to solidify the role of general councils beyond the extraordinary situation of the schism. A decree often paired with *Haec sancta synodus* is *Frequens*, which predated the papal election of Martin V by a month. *Frequens* stated a general council should always be either in session or expected soon. The statement mandated a general council to meet five years after the end of Constance, then seven years after that one, and then once every ten years in perpetuity. The pope and cardinals could shorten the time between councils, but they could never lengthen the gap. In addition, the delegates required all new popes to pledge their acceptance of general councils. As it finished its business in 1418, Constance clearly tried to make general councils a regular feature of the church's life and administration.

Basel-Ferrara-Florence-Rome

In compliance with *Frequens*, Martin V called a council that met in Pavia and Siena (1423–24), but like Pisa this meeting did not make the standard list of twenty-one general councils. Though he owed his election to Constance, Martin V was no conciliarist. His goal, and the goal of Eugene IV, who succeeded him as pope in 1431, was to recover and strengthen papal authority by signing agreements with other monarchs, who in effect recognized him as the church's head.

Eugene IV, also no friend of general councils, nevertheless followed *Frequens* and called the next meeting, which has made the standard list. This general council met in several different places. At a critical point, one group of delegates broke off from the rest and claimed its meeting was the authentic council, while another group in a separate city said the same thing. Scholars sometimes disagree in their interpretation of this meeting because of its confusing events, but they generally refer to it as the council of Basel-Ferrara-Florence-Rome (1431–45).

Pope Eugene IV had only reluctantly called a general council at Basel in July 1431. Because attendance was sparse at first, he decided to dissolve the gathering that December. But the delegates, surprisingly led by Eugene's own papal legate and most of his cardinals, did not leave Basel and instead reacted forcefully. They summoned the pope to Basel and demanded he withdraw his statement of dissolution. They also said that if the pope died, no election could take place outside the general council. Those who elected the new pope must swear to obey the general council if selected for the papal throne. The Basel delegates went further, stating a pope could not dissolve or move a general council without their approval; then they reaffirmed *Frequens*.

Because Eugene IV was in a weak political position and many countries supported Basel, he had to comply with this resurgence of conciliarism. He acknowledged in December 1433 that the council currently meeting in Basel had been legitimate since its beginning in July 1431. The council had won a victory and made a point of restating *Haec sancta synodus* in 1434 verbatim, an action it had taken once before, in 1432, after Eugene said Basel was dissolved and while the delegates were fighting for their meeting's life. Two years later, in 1436, Basel continued to proclaim its conciliar principles. The delegates required new popes to promise to keep holding general councils. To counter the possibility of selective papal memories, they required popes to be reminded of this promise each year on the anniversary of their election or consecration.

After these events, in 1438 the council took up other topics on its agenda, yet the context remained the papal-conciliar power struggle. The main item of business was an attempt to reconcile the eastern and western churches, an effort that returned to Lyons II's deliberations. The issue became part of the battle between Basel and Eugene IV. Each side, pope and general council, wanted to represent the west in deliberations with the east (called "the Greeks" in the documents), because that would implicitly mean it had the authority to speak for the Latin church. Whoever ended up as the institution with which the Greeks dealt could then claim superiority over the other.

A debate followed about the location of the meeting with the easterners. Most of the general council voted for Basel, Avignon, or Savoy and made a point of saying that not even a pope could override this vote. Eugene IV, along with a minority of the delegates, preferred Florence, which is where the west eventually met with the Greeks. The easterners may have decided on the papal meeting for three reasons. First, it was easier to deal with one authority (the papacy) rather than Basel's more disparate conciliar elements; second, the pope agreed to pay all of their expenses to travel to Italy and stay there; third, eastern leaders feared Muslim attacks and needed western aid immediately. They probably thought the prospects of financial and military support were greater from the pope than the council.

The majority-minority disagreement at Basel split the council. Eugene IV moved what he considered the lawful general council from Basel to Ferrara, and then to Florence in 1439. In the meantime, a group of delegates remained in Basel and maintained that their meeting, not the pope's, was the true continuation of the general council of Basel. Eugene IV responded with several negative references to the delegates in 1438 and 1439. They remained in Basel, the pope stated, "without any authority" and were a "faction of agitators." He said the gathering at Basel "is and ought to be considered a spurious gathering and conventicle, and can in no way exist with the authority of a general council." The pope excommunicated the remaining delegates and ordered them to disperse or risk being thrown out of Basel, but they continued to meet until 1449.

Before we return to this "rump" council in Basel, we must look at the chief development at Florence in 1439: the attempt to unify the church's eastern and western halves. There were several theological and liturgical points up for discussion that, in some cases, returned to questions earlier councils had addressed: Were souls in purgatory purified by fire? Should leavened or unleavened bread be used for the Eucharist? What was the nature and jurisdiction of papal primacy? Did the Holy Spirit proceed from the Father and the Son *(filioque),* as westerners held, or from the Father only, as easterners generally believed?

After much debate and deadlock, these matters were settled by compromises that, as it turned out, did not last. The two sides agreed some souls were purified by fire in purgatory and that leavened bread was permitted for the east while unleavened bread continued as the western tradition. One of the more contentious issues was *filioque.* Easterners resisted the west's addition of *filioque* to the creed by returning to an earlier argument: The general councils of Ephesus and Chalcedon had already forbidden any additions to the ancient councils' creeds, which did not include this Latin word. Eventually, however, east and west decided that the Greek and Latin fathers to whom they looked for evidence of one position or the other had essentially agreed the Holy Spirit proceeds from Father and Son. As the statement of union phrased it in a diplomatic attempt to satisfy everyone: "All were aiming at the same meaning in different words." Finally, after difficult discussions the Greeks accepted papal primacy—including the statement that popes have "full power of tending, ruling, and governing the whole church"—but their agreement, as with the other major issues, was delicate at best.

The eastern and western delegates announced their reunion in a decree written in both Greek and Latin, appropriately titled in Latin *Laetentur coeli* ("Let the heavens rejoice!"). The joy was short-lived and, as had occurred after Lyons II, failure replaced the initial optimism when it quickly became clear the agreements would not stick. Greek delegates began arguing about what had happened as soon as they returned home, and the eastern emperor did not promulgate *Laetentur coeli.* The delegates at Florence and the pope had not learned the lessons of Lyons II and its aftermath. In the interest of declaring union, they did not deal comprehensively with subjects that had long histories of complicated ecclesiastical politics and nuanced theology. East and west remained split.

As these events played out in the east, in the west the general council that had started at Basel and then moved to Ferrara and Florence kept meeting. Eugene IV's council negotiated statements of unity with other Christian groups: Armenians in 1439, Copts in 1442, Syrians in 1444, and Chaldeans and Maronites in 1445. The fact that Eugene IV could reach settlements with them solidified his papal claim, as opposed to a general council's, to represent the church. Eugene's council moved in 1443 to Rome, where it held several more sessions. The last one met in 1445, but no document officially declared the end of the long, tumultuous general council of Basel-Ferrara-Florence-Rome.

Meanwhile, back in Basel, the delegates who had refused to move to Ferrara and then Florence kept meeting and claiming their gathering, not Eugene IV's, was the valid general council. Their statements became more extreme as they expressed and exercised conciliar principles in strong terms, which led to the steady decline of secular support. They declared the idea that a general council was higher than the pope, the heart of *Haec sancta synodus,* to be an article of the Christian faith. In 1439, they "deposed" Eugene IV and elected a new pope, who took the name Felix V. Ironically, conciliarism had achieved its greatest success at Constance when that council's conclave elected Martin V to end the Great Western Schism in 1417. Barely two decades later, another general council (or, more properly according to history and the church's judgment, a group claiming the authority of a general council) recreated schism through this election of Felix V, who is recorded as an antipope.

The response from Eugene IV was direct and unambiguous: He commanded Felix V to abandon his claim to the papacy and acknowledge Eugene as true pope. With hardly any backing left and even Felix V wavering, in 1449 the remnant at Basel decided to end things. They "elected" as pope Nicholas V, who in fact had been reigning as Eugene IV's successor for several years. In the interest of peace, Nicholas V accepted Felix's "abdication" in 1449 and named him a cardinal. The little left of this council at Basel then voted itself out of existence.

Conciliarism's Legacy

Looking back from the end of this part of the story, conciliarism probably constitutes the most interesting chapter in the history of general councils. But it seems to have played itself out by
the middle of the fifteenth century. Conciliarism had flourished
during the crisis of the schism, which made the papal position
weak, but it faltered in its own extremism and in the face of the
papal recovery of power under Martin V and Eugene IV. Conciliar
ideas remained in the air, however, to such an extent that a later
pope, Pius II, felt compelled to issue a condemnation of conciliarism, called *Execrabilis,* in 1460.

Pius II, a former conciliarist, went straight after conciliarism's
central principle. He said some people "imbued with a spirit of
rebellion" claimed it was permissible to appeal over a pope's head
to a general council. Calling this idea "a horrible abuse" and "a
deadly poison," he condemned such appeals, calling them "erro-
neous and abominable...null and void." Conciliarism was not
completely dead, though, and its fifteenth-century examples of
challenging papal authority would have great implications for the
sixteenth century.

The fate of conciliarism was not the only legacy of the turbu-
lent fifteenth-century general councils. Another had to do with
reforms that were absolutely necessary but never made substantial
progress. The topic of reform had been overlooked while general
councils and popes fought for power. As a result, Constance and
Basel-Ferrara-Florence-Rome failed to fix troubles the church simply had to face: worldliness, simony, greed, ambition, pluralism
and absenteeism, poor clerical training, and bishops interested in
everything except shepherding their dioceses.

Constance and the various stages of Basel had legislated some
reforms, but popes and bishops mainly ignored them—or, at best,
took very small steps to correct the mounting abuses in the dioceses and parishes of Christianity. At Constance, delegates turned
their attention to improving priestly education, morality, and service—especially on the parish level. But these ideas remained proposals and died in committee because the issue of reuniting the

papacy dominated the council. Constance did successfully legislate some reforms in the church's higher levels: The delegates voted to curb simony and heavy taxation, particularly connected to the papacy. Two decades later, the Basel sessions battling Eugene IV in 1433 through 1435 addressed papal abuses by restricting (and in some cases outlawing) the high revenues and fees the papacy demanded when appointing many church officials.

But Basel's reforms, like Constance's before them, languished because popes were interested in demonstrating the papacy's ultimate power in the church. Fifteenth-century popes after Constance and Basel-Ferrara-Florence-Rome were not about to follow those general councils' rules. Although the fifteenth-century councils may have thrilled some Christians, real problems in the church that required attention grew as popes and general councils competed. Because reforms were not put into place, the church would soon need more general councils, especially after a theology professor named Martin Luther proposed some striking approaches to the church's problems.

Chapter 8
Reform Lost
and Regained:
Lateran V (1512–1517)
and Trent (1545–1563)

The sixteenth century witnessed two general councils. Lateran V
was a long but fruitless meeting that ended just months before a
famous invitation to deal with the church's real problems: Luther's
95 Theses in 1517. Trent met nearly thirty years later in three sets of
sessions spread out from 1545 to 1563. At Trent, the Roman
church not only had to reexplain her own doctrines, but also deal
with the consequences of several centuries of failed attempts to
reform the church. More than at any other moment in the church's
life, at Trent the church had to look at herself and recognize that the
troubles she faced were partially her own fault. It was a moment as
critical in the church's life as the challenge to write doctrinal creeds
had been for the general councils of the first millennium.

Lateran V

At the dawn of the sixteenth century, the church had big problems. But Pope Julius II, known as the warrior pope because he literally led armies in battle, only assembled Lateran V (1512–17) because he had to. His enemies had called their own council at Pisa, a location with many bad memories for the church from the schism. Some dissatisfied cardinals had won the support of the French king and the Holy Roman emperor for this gathering at Pisa, which met from late 1511 to early 1512. While rather small, the assembly caused trouble for Julius II. Like Basel, it suspended the pope and asserted, once more, Constance's declaration of conciliar supremacy. Conciliarism again challenged the papacy.

The combative Julius II responded by calling his own council for 1512, which he intended to wrap with the mantle of the first four Lateran councils from the high Middle Ages. Like them, Lateran V was a very papal council: The sessions met in the pope's building, and its documents took the form of papal bulls. The first order of business was obvious: The pope condemned the meeting at Pisa, calling it a "quasi-council" and "counterfeit," and its participants "schismatics and heretics." Eventually, both the French king and the Holy Roman emperor repudiated the meeting at Pisa and supported Lateran V, which continued to meet after Julius II died in February 1513. Leo X was elected as his successor within a month, and Lateran V continued with little interruption.

After condemning the meeting at Pisa, the second major task for Lateran V was fighting off a legal document known as the *Pragmatic Sanction of Bourges*. Dating to 1438 from France, the *Pragmatic Sanction* supported Constance and Basel's conciliar principles as contained in *Haec sancta synodus* and *Frequens*. It also restricted the pope's power to name bishops, abbots, and other church officials by asserting such officials should be elected by those over whom the official would have power.

Lateran V called the document an attack on the papacy and ordered copies of the *Pragmatic Sanction* destroyed. The papacy was so preoccupied with conciliarism that Lateran V condemned the *Pragmatic Sanction,* and the conciliar threat it represented, not once but twice: under Julius II in 1512 and again under Leo X in 1516. Leo X's statement, known as *Pastor aeternus*, underlined the fact that general councils must meet and act only under papal approval and with great respect for the papacy.

The agenda also included reform. Lateran V was not unaware of what needed fixing, especially after Giles of Viterbo, the head of the Augustinian order, gave a candid account of the church's troubles to open the council in 1512. What was needed more than anything else right now was renewal, he told the council, and Lateran V was just the place to start. As Giles of Viterbo put it,

> ...[T]he church cannot perform well without the attention of councils....[W]ith the light of councils and the holy spirit, the winds blow and the dead eyes of the church come to life again and receive the light....[W]ithout councils, faith cannot stand firm. Without councils, therefore, we cannot be saved.

With rhetorical flourishes, he asked a series of hard questions to lay the church's problems before the council.

> When has ambition been more unrestrained, greed more burning? When has the license to sin been more shameless? When has the temerity in speaking, in arguing, in writing against piety been more common or more unafraid? When has there been among the people not only a greater neglect, but a greater contempt for the sacred, for the sacraments, for the keys [of forgiveness of sins], and for the holy commandments? When have our religion and faith been more open to the derision even of the lowest classes?

Lateran V has been criticized for its failure to institute effective reforms, but the council did legislate against simony, concubinage, and usury in addition to lay control of church money, property, and rights. Cardinals were ordered to live in unassuming and spare households. The council warned against false preachers, fake miracles, sorcery, and blasphemy. It also required oversight of printed material like books and pamphlets, which were proliferating in affordable copies because of the printing press Gutenberg had perfected about fifty years earlier. Lateran V was concerned with errors against the Christian faith being spread this way—a worry that, according to Catholics, proved correct when Protestants made good use of the new technology to disseminate their ideas through the penny press just a few years later.

The difficulty lay not so much in the attention Lateran V gave to reform, but in how it wrote its rules. A leading scholar of this general council noted its speakers' frankness about the church's state, especially in the highest levels. But this same scholar concluded the council built so many loopholes into its reforms that it proved easy to avoid the restrictions. At bottom, the papacy, cardinals, and curia simply had no interest in real reform: Curial officials depended so heavily on financial improprieties that opposition to reform was firmly entrenched.

Moreover, these curial officials, who were mostly Italian bishops, dominated the council so much that Lateran V can barely be called ecumenical. There was one notable exception: For the first time in the history of the general councils a bishop represented the "New World" that Christopher Columbus had encountered just two decades before. That bishop was from Santo Domingo in the Caribbean. But he, too, was an Italian.

The members of Lateran V could not have known, as they left Rome in the spring of 1517, that before the year was out Martin Luther would stir up ideas, emotions, and movements that would change Christianity as it had never been changed before. But we must remember one of the reasons why the conversation Luther started became so virulent so quickly: The Roman church had not attended to important issues and had dug herself into a very large hole. Reform had gone lacking for more than a century, and so tensions bubbled to an increasingly higher boil until Luther's *95 Theses* provided the critical mass for them to explode.

The Protestant Context

While this history of the general councils is not the place to describe the range of Protestant ideas in that explosion, a general sense of the diverse Protestant movements will allow us to see what

Trent faced when it finally met. A wide assortment of Protestant ideas in different countries represented diverse forms of addressing the Roman church's problems.

As at Constance, Basel, and Lateran V, some Catholic leaders saw the necessity of reform and the need for a thorough house cleaning, especially in the papacy and curia. But a number of Protestant groups had a completely different idea of reform: They did not believe the Roman church's doctrines, hierarchy, and rituals required reforming or fixing per se. Because most Protestant groups did not believe these Catholic things belonged in the church in the first place, they wanted Christians to throw them out completely and return to what, according to them, Jesus had intended from the very beginning. For this reason, Protestantism is sometimes referred to as more a revolution than a reform movement.

Calvinism provides a good example of this fundamental opposition to Roman church structures, as opposed to the Catholic desire to keep but repair them. Jean Calvin and his sixteenth-century followers saw the early Christian community described in the Acts of the Apostles as the model to resurrect. They wanted to restore the offices they read about in Acts: deacons, teachers, pastors, and elders. This approach wiped out bishops as Catholics knew them and certainly the papacy, college of cardinals, and curia. They also found in Acts precedents for a more participatory form of church government that leaned toward the medieval conciliarism that had lived its greatest moment at Constance. So the fifteenth-century conciliar challenge to papal authority, especially at Constance and the more radical element at Basel, became part of Protestantism's context, too.

As a consequence, in the sixteenth century the Roman church faced objections to her core ideas and structures from several fronts. Luther, Calvin, and others questioned the very foundations of the Roman church. It was as if people wondered anew just what the Christian church was, what she believed, and how her members practiced their faith. Fundamental questions flowed naturally from Luther's starting points. What are the sources of authority: scripture and/or tradition? And what is tradition: the writings of the fathers and/or general councils and/or papal decrees? How many sacraments are there, what do they mean, and what do they do? Who decides these matters and on what grounds do they base their explanation? How should the church run herself and celebrate her beliefs liturgically?

Trent

With such a major challenge taking place on such a large scale, why did it take almost three decades after Luther's first steps in 1517 for Trent to start meeting? The Protestant desire for a council dampened Catholic enthusiasm because the Roman church did not want to look like she was giving in to her critics. Protestants wanted everyone, clergy and lay, to participate in a council; they sought the backing of secular powers to establish one, preferably in Germany. Moreover, Lutherans and other Protestants believed Christians could call a council on their own and did not want papal interference. They also knew popes would not readily call a council because the papal curia comprised one of the main elements in the church needing an overhaul. It was also true that not every pope in this period was happy with the idea of a general council, however much it was needed. This may have been because conciliarism's challenge to papal authority had dovetailed with the Protestant attack on the very concept of the papacy.

A Catholic council had to deal with this unprecedented context and face some basic and crucial questions about the church's life. Eventually, after some hesitant steps and objections, the organizers selected the city of Trent, which was then on imperial soil but today is in northeast Italy (near modern Switzerland and Austria). Finally, the long awaited and extremely essential Catholic general council would meet both to take up problems that predated the Protestants and to respond to the developments in Christianity since Luther opened the floodgates of questions for the Roman Catholic Church.

Trent met in three stages: 1545 through 1548, 1551 through 1552, and 1562 through 1563. There are many reasons for this broken chronology, but the most important have to do with the facts that the agenda was enormous and complicated and the times were dangerous. Not only did Catholics have to discuss and implement useful reforms; they had to explain the Roman church's teachings on the core issues the Protestants had questioned (especially authority, tradition, and sacraments) fully, carefully, and effectively. And many of these discussions took place while religious and political wars were being fought all over Europe. When the second stage adjourned in 1552, for instance, the bishops planned only a two-year suspension, but a decade passed before Trent could resume.

As we turn to Trent's debates and decisions, we must remember that each of the council's three stages had its own dynamics, controversies, and stories. But it is more helpful for our purposes to gather together the central subjects that occupied Trent's three stages. Because of the contentiousness of several topics, final decisions were sometimes postponed from one stage to the next. We will look at four major subjects: the authority of scripture and tradition, the role of bishops, doctrines and sacraments, and reforms.

The first of Trent's four main subjects concerned the authority of scripture and tradition. Here the Catholics and Protestants faced a basic disagreement because they had different answers to the crucial questions: "What is authority, and who says so?" This foundational difference concerning the authority of scripture alone or the authority of both scripture and tradition underlay every other discussion. All explanations of doctrine (and, indeed, of all church matters) had to rest on some authority. If the two sides disagreed about this first principle—that is, the very nature and sources of authority—then no progress could be made on any other topics.

Simply put, most Protestants believed all Christians could interpret scripture for themselves and that scripture should be the ultimate authority in the church—although different Protestant groups assigned varying levels of importance to Christianity's great thinkers and councils, especially those dating back to the early church, which they esteemed so highly. Catholics, in contrast, said the church, in particular the top of her hierarchy, should over-see scriptural interpretation and that individual Christians could not interpret scripture on their own.

The Catholic position also held that the church's authority rested not only on scripture, but also on tradition. This tradition included the writings of the fathers, papal statements, and concil-iar documents—all guided by the Holy Spirit. The Catholic idea of authority relied on the church's hierarchy as the agent having the right and power to decide what was to be included and excluded from scripture and tradition. Catholics believed this teaching authority had been handed down to the hierarchy over the cen-turies in an unbroken succession. That line of succession started with the apostles and moved through the fathers and bishops up to, and including, the members of the Council of Trent.

From these starting points concerning the authority of scrip-ture and tradition as interpreted by the Catholic hierarchy, Trent began with the basics. The delegates issued a creed very early on, in 1546, which repeated the ancient formulas set down by the fathers at Nicaea I in 325 and Constantinople I in 381. Throughout the rest of its documents and especially its doctrinal statements, Trent always made sure it demonstrated its own authority and the sources of that authority. The fathers at Trent did so by continually stressing that their teachings rested on scripture and tradition, especially as that tradition was found in—and handed down by— the fathers and the councils.

Because of the central importance the word of God played in the Protestant reformations and the Catholic responses, Trent turned to the Latin, or Vulgate, Bible. After listing the books of the Vulgate Bible, Trent called for a fresh version of the Latin text. But the fathers at Trent also made a point of saying only the Roman church, not individual Christians, could interpret that Bible with final authority.

The second major issue for Trent stemmed from the first: the bishops' teaching authority as members of the church's hierarchy. The subject had particular importance in light of the Protestant questioning of the offices of bishop and pope. This context resulted in Trent's strong reaction against this Protestant challenge and helped make Trent a very episcopal general council. Trent revolved around bishops much more than the fifteenth-century general councils had. At Constance and Basel-Ferrara-Florence-Rome, nonepiscopal theologians and canon lawyers sometimes eclipsed the bishops. At Trent, by contrast, votes were restricted to bishops, the generals of religious orders, and representatives of monasteries. Although bishops could bring theologians with them as consultants and send proxies in their own places, these theologians and proxies could not vote for themselves or in the names of their bishops.

Looking beyond the council's eventual adjournment, Trent reasserted the leadership role of the bishop, especially the bishop who headed a diocese: He connected the church's head (papacy, college of cardinals, and curia) with her body (dioceses and parishes). More than any other figure, the bishop emerged from Trent as the major player in reinvigorating the sixteenth-century Catholic Church tested on so many fronts, inside and out. Trent frequently laid on the bishops' shoulders the substantial burden of implementing the reforms for clergy and laity that it legislated. The major way of overseeing reform required the bishop to visit his diocese frequently and inquire what the clergy were teaching and preaching, how the faithful were responding, how parishes were celebrating the sacraments, and how both clergy and laity were living according to the moral standards the church set. Trent also charged bishops with carefully examining men to be ordained priests and making sure they possessed proper theological training along with appropriate spiritual and moral qualities.

Above all, Trent reiterated the jurisdiction and dignity of the priesthood and, especially, the episcopacy. Only the pope could judge a bishop charged with major crimes or heresy; lesser cases could come before a provincial synod. The council was concerned not only with civil authorities reaching into church affairs, but also with bishops who let this happen. Trent declared it

> can only be deeply saddened on hearing that some bishops forget their standing and seriously dishonor pontifical dignity in that they behave with unfitting subservience towards royal ministers,

rulers and barons, in church and out of it, and, as if they themselves were lowly altar servers, not only give them an undeserved
precedence but even act personally as their servants.

To work against this situation, Trent renewed all prior rules supporting episcopal dignity and arguing against subservience to civil
authorities. This mandate brings to mind several regulations from
the first millennium's general councils, especially Constantinople
IV, which nearly seven hundred years before acted against rumors
of government officials dressing up like priests and bishops and
holding "pretend" liturgies.

The third major subject for Trent was doctrine. In order to
fight Protestant ideas, Catholics had to state just what the church
believed. The bishops at Trent began, logically, with original sin
and then moved to the concept of justification—two ideas at the
core of Christian theology. Trent's bishops stressed that the original sin of Adam marked each soul, which consequently had to be
wiped clean by baptism. This statement went against a variety of
Protestant ideas, some of which said that Adam's action led only to
a predisposition toward sin among God's people and that Adam
did not taint anyone but himself. In terms of justification, which
most Protestant groups thought of as based on faith alone, Trent
reiterated the central importance of good works, in addition to
faith, which acted in cooperation with divine grace.

Treating original sin and justification required Trent to discuss
sacraments, too. Diverse Protestant groups, to varying degrees, had
denied the sacramental status of most Catholic sacraments (marriage, confirmation, confession, extreme unction, and holy orders)
and had assigned different explanations to the others they retained
(baptism and Eucharist). Trent's bishops carefully named and
defined the Catholic Church's seven sacraments as baptism, confirmation, Eucharist, penance, last anointing, holy orders, and marriage. They described why and how each was a sacrament along
with each sacrament's effect on the believer.

Along with original sin, justification, and the number and
meaning of the seven Catholic sacraments, Trent had to take on a
major issue concerning one sacrament about which even Protestants

disagreed: What was the Eucharist? Some Protestants believed the bread and wine remained bread and wine, but also really turned into Jesus' body and blood (consubstantiation). Other Protestants said Jesus' body and blood were never truly present at all, but that the bread and wine were only symbols of Jesus and the "Lord's Supper" (as these Protestants tended to call it) was a memorial of the Last Supper and not a sacrifice.

Trent reached back to the word "transubstantiation," which Lateran IV had used in 1215. The Catholic belief said Jesus' body and blood were truly present in the Eucharist. The mass was really a sacrifice and not just a memorial. Moreover, the real presence of Christ remained after mass concluded, which allowed Catholics to reserve the Eucharist in tabernacles and to expose the Eucharist in monstrances for adoration, processions, and benediction outside mass. As for the liturgy itself, the bishops upheld the mass but noted it should be explained to the congregants. In addition, Trent said the bishops should oversee the translation of the Latin rituals surrounding the sacraments into the vernacular language and should make sure priests and bishops explained them to the laity according to the council's definitions.

The last of Trent's four major subjects dealt with the broad reforms that were necessary, but that prior councils had failed to design and implement very well—if at all. These reforms touched on nearly every aspect of the church's life from top to bottom.

One preeminent group of reforms dealt with priests and the people they served. Trent reasserted the importance of preaching: priests were told to preach every Sunday and feast day. Provisions were made to improve the priests' own knowledge of scripture so they could adequately share it with their parishioners; there would also be help for priests who struggled with illiteracy. Trent permitted bishops to suspend "unsuitable and incompetent" ministers and three times warned against itinerant preachers who were not subject to any bishop or religious superior's authority. Bishops were directed to hold diocesan synods annually, with groups of neighboring dioceses required to meet in provincial synods once every three years. They also had to step up visits around their dioceses.

These rules are a reminder that the earliest councils also wanted to see frequent meetings between bishops and their communities so problems on the parochial and diocesan levels could be faced before they got worse. Diocesan and provincial synods also provided the best place to start ordering, implementing, and monitoring Trent's reform program.

An important element of reform in the area of priests and parishes was Trent's establishment of seminaries to train priests. Although there were some precursors for these separate places to form ministers spiritually and intellectually, seminaries in their modern form date back only to 1563. Trent's bishops gave guidelines concerning what the candidates for priesthood should study, what the qualifications of their professors should be, how to pay for the seminary, and what procedures to use in examining men seeking ordination.

Other reforms took aim at the worldliness and greed that had plagued the church for centuries. With different levels of strength and effectiveness, Trent legislated against simony, concubinage, nepotism, and hereditary benefices. Any priest charged with the care of souls, such as the pastor of a parish or the bishop of a diocese, was ordered to live with his people; this rule confronted the long-standing twin problems of pluralism and absenteeism. The council also wanted bishops to be sure there were enough parishes of appropriate size to meet parishioners' sacramental and spiritual needs. Like earlier councils in the Middle Ages, Trent also required clergy to wear modest clothing and to behave in a suitably moral manner so they would provide proper examples, in word and deed, for their parishioners to follow.

Another group of reforms dealt with sensitive issues: indulgences, relics, saints, images, and purgatory. Many Protestants had challenged these beliefs and practices, all extremely popular aspects of Catholic devotions. Some Protestants objected to the communion of saints and the idea of purgatory because they seemed to place humans (especially Mary) on the same level as God. Also, these devotions contributed to a certain mathematical spirituality and gave money a potentially insidious role in piety.

Christians were multiplying the number of prayers they said or relics they touched, thinking this would automatically increase their holiness and decrease their time in purgatory. Sometimes they simply bought the spiritual benefits (indulgences) of good acts, such as pilgrimages, without actually performing them.

In response, but without saying so, Trent bowed to Martin Luther's very loud criticism of indulgence peddlers, against whom Lateran IV had warned 350 years before. Trent abolished both the title and the job of "alms collector." The council retained indulgences but said Christians should use them only for devotional purposes, not private financial gain. Trent also retained the communion and intercession of saints, veneration for their relics and images, and the idea of purgatory, even as it nodded (but did not concede) to the accurate Protestant criticisms of arithmetical piety. The council said Christians should exercise these beliefs and devotions properly, but it noted specifically when treating purgatory that bishops "should prohibit all that panders to curiosity and superstition, or smacks of base gain, as scandalous stumbling-blocks to the faithful." Trent reminded Christians that Nicaea II had already taught about the proper use of images when it discussed the errors of the iconoclasts in 787. Moreover, the bishops were given the duty to review new images, relics, or miracles, none of which Christians could revere without the church's approval.

After Trent

Like its predecessors, the general council of Trent was not just an event, but a set of documents that required implementation once the meeting ended. This exercise was more critical and difficult after Trent than after prior general councils because Europe was still dealing with the unparalleled split between Catholics and Protestants. Oversight of the council and of Catholic writings became crucial, especially as the Protestant groups had so successfully used the new technology of the printing press to spread their competing religious beliefs.

The Catholic Church took two major steps to control Trent's implementation. Trent said the Roman church, usually in the person of the local bishop, should watch over the publication of books on sacred topics. This supervision harkened back to Lateran V's similar statement just before Protestant writings began to circulate in affordable vernacular pamphlets.

The second major step was Pope Pius IV's announcement that no one could interpret Trent's decrees or publish explanations or clarifications without Rome's approval. One of the pope's first actions after Trent adjourned involved naming a group of cardinals to assess questions about Trent's statements and mediate disputes that might come up about how to put Trent into practice in diverse or new contexts. This centralized office, which came to be known as the Congregation on the Council, was new in the history of the general councils. According to recent scholarship, the congregation ended up not spreading Trent's ideas as much as restricting some of the council's innovative elements. Those forward-looking tendencies (teaching in the vernacular, its many pastoral and spiritual reforms) were replaced over time with a rigorism that was not intended by Trent's bishops, but which has tainted the council's reputation.

In fact, our contemporary understanding of Trent has been the subject of a new wave of reassessment, especially in light of Vatican II. The recent rediscovery of Trent as it really was, and not a caricature, constitutes an important development in the history of the general councils. Before leaving Trent, we should look at the current reevaluation of this council, which is so often placed in opposition to Vatican II. In truth, Trent may be the least understood and most attacked council of the church's twenty-one general councils.

A dark cloud often settles over the popular picture of the council of Trent because of the resounding phrase *anathema sit* ("let him be anathema")—that is, let whoever holds an opinion contrary to Catholic teaching be cursed and excommunicated. This phrase makes it sound as if the members of Trent sat around all day and simply shot down Protestant ideas, which they defined as heresies.

The phrase *anathema sit* does appear with some frequency in the council's documents, but the council did not start with condemnations. Rather, the council first laid down what the Catholic Church taught on certain matters—justification, for example, or Eucharist and the mass. Then, out of a concern to point out where Catholics and Protestants disagreed, the members listed the positions others held and said these positions and the people holding them ought to be condemned: *anathema sit*. This procedure reminds us of the doctrinal councils of the first millennium, which often listed both what the church taught as truth along with what other people, those the councils now declared to be heretics, taught as falsehood.

Because Trent took so much time and effort to define just what the Catholic Church did and did not teach, the question has come up whether Trent was doing something new or old. Did the members simply restate in old words or reassert in new words the long-standing doctrines of the church? Because of the Protestant questions and teachings, did the Catholics have to rethink, reformulate, and perhaps expand doctrines that had not been adequately explained or thought through in the past?

Trent had to address the questions Protestants had raised in the minds of some Catholics, but the council was not original in the sense that its members made up entirely new doctrines completely divorced from the church's tradition. In fact, the statement on penance makes a point of saying the Catholic teaching differs from that of the "innovators," clearly a negative reference charging Protestant theologians with being cut off from the past. On the other hand, it cannot be denied that Trent finally created clarity by synthesizing and systematizing diverse medieval theological treatments of the topics under discussion. One of Trent's achievements was its overall success in stating just what the Roman church taught about essential items of Christian faith and Catholic practice more conclusively, systematically, and precisely than ever before. Trent was also innovative and open in its establishment of seminaries and its endorsement of expanded vernacular catechesis. To this degree, Trent did not simply react to Protestantism—

though, of course, it met in large part to respond to Protestant ideas, questions, and criticisms.

Trent remained a touchstone for the Catholic Church because it was the last general council before modern times. The interval between the end of Trent in 1563 and the start of the next general council, Vatican I in 1869, takes up 306 years. That is the longest span between general councils in church history—nearly as long as it took after Jesus' death and resurrection to call the first general council, Nicaea I, in 325. So whether we judge its drawn-out sessions favorably or not, as active or reactive, as conservative or progressive, it remains true that the Council of Trent left its mark on the church for centuries.

BIBLIOGRAPHY

C. M. D. Crowder, ed. *Unity, Heresy, and Reform, 1378–1460*. London: Edward Arnold, 1977.

Joseph Gill. *The Council of Florence*. Cambridge: Cambridge University Press, 1959.

Hubert Jedin. *A History of the Council of Trent*. Translated by Ernest Graf. St. Louis: Herder, 1957.

Carter Lindberg. *The European Reformations*. Oxford: Blackwell, 1996.

Nelson H. Minnich. *The Fifth Lateran Council (1512–17)*. Brookfield Vt.: Ashgate Publishing Company, 1993.

Francis Oakley. *The Western Church in the Later Middle Ages*. Ithaca, N.Y.: Cornell University Press, 1979.

John W. O'Malley. *Trent and All That: Renaming Catholicism in the Early Modern Era*. Cambridge, Mass.: Harvard University Press, 2000.

Joachim W. Stieber. *Pope Eugenius IV, the Council of Basel, and the Secular and Ecclesiastical Authorities in the Empire: The Conflict over Supreme Authority and Power in the Church*. Leiden: E. J. Brill, 1978.

Phillip H. Stump. *The Reforms of the Council of Constance (1414–1418)*. Leiden: E. J. Brill, 1994.

Brian Tierney. *Foundations of the Conciliar Theory*. Cambridge: Cambridge University Press, 1955; new ed., Leiden: E. J. Brill, 1998.

Part IV

COUNCILS IN THE MODERN AGE

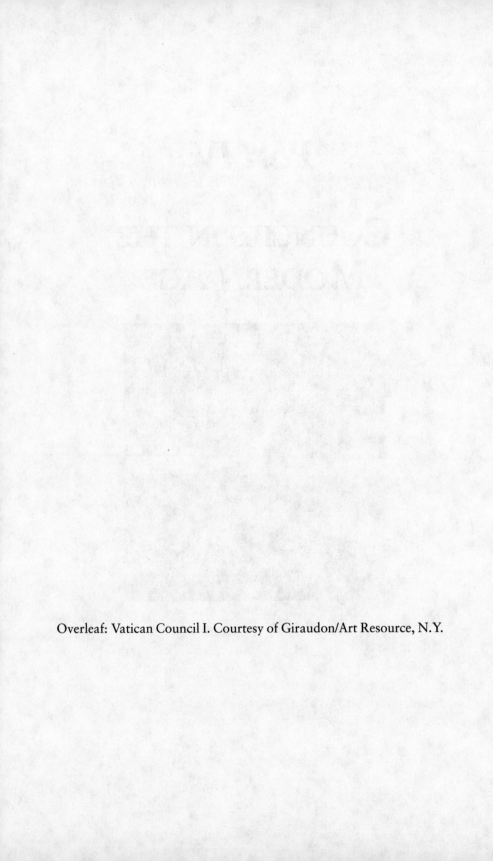

Overleaf: Vatican Council I. Courtesy of Giraudon/Art Resource, N.Y.

The world during the three centuries between Trent and Vatican I expanded in many significant ways. Even before Luther and Trent, increasing encounters with unfamiliar civilizations around the globe forced open Europe's myopia. In the two centuries after Trent adjourned in 1563, the Scientific Revolution and the Enlightenment pushed faith to the side, challenging religion with rationalism, secularism, and a more individualistic mentality. At the end of the eighteenth century, the American and French revolutions attacked monarchies and aristocracies. Traditionalists supported their positions with claims to divine rights and blue blood, while the revolutionaries wanted self-determining democracies and republics built upon civil liberties. In the nineteenth century, nationalism swept Europe and competed with religious identity and affiliation for a citizen's ultimate loyalty. And it is not an exaggeration to say the twentieth century witnessed some of the most advanced and breathless developments in technology, media, economics, education, politics, and social status the planet had ever seen.

Though she lived within this landscape of change, the church tended to step away from modern developments that endangered her. In the worst cases, this translated into a perception of a church hidden away from the world, afraid of rapid changes in industry and politics, and generally distrustful of modernity. This picture is not entirely true: liturgical, spiritual, and theological renewal progressed with great health and excitement on the level of dioceses and parishes. But the portrait of Rome and her curial chain of command as intransigent is not entirely false, either.

The church did not call a general council between Trent's conclusion in 1563 and Vatican I's opening in 1869. At least initially, this may be due to the fact that the church was sifting through and implementing Trent—a daunting task liturgically, doctrinally, and geographically. But over time, the gap between general councils may also have been connected to a political development, since constitutionalism was continually confronting monarchies in early modern Europe.

Citizens' sovereignty and relative social equality were cutting-edge ideas in government and society that spilled into church matters. Not long before Trent, conciliarism had favored greater representation and decisive control of the church. Conciliarism's history might have led some to think of a church council as equivalent to the secular parliaments gaining popularity. So constitutionalism attacked the institutional church, especially in Rome, for the same reasons it fought other monarchies and aristocracies. But monarchs did not always unite to support one another. Napoleon famously bullied Popes Pius VI and Pius VII at the turn of the nineteenth century, even holding Pius VII captive. As far as the papacy was concerned, it was not a time for councils.

After the church went more than three centuries without a general council, however, Pope Pius IX—usually known by the Italian name Pio Nono—called Vatican I, mainly to deal with an important question given these political and social developments. More than anything else, he wanted papal infallibility defined and proclaimed at this meeting. Such a statement, he felt, would send out a clear message to all who thought of the church as a republic and the papacy as just another monarchy. Papal infallibility is an important statement, but commentators often overlook the deliberations that took place to refine its definition. These debates tell us much about the state of general councils, papal authority, and episcopal collegiality in the nineteenth-century church, while also revealing that Vatican I did not resolve every aspect of these topics.

Like the general councils of the first millennium, many of which dealt with issues treated only partially by prior councils, Vatican II picked up some unanswered questions from Trent and Vatican I. But Vatican II did not just continue unfinished business. It was a very different general council called for a very different reason in a very different world.

Chapter 9
Papal Infallibility:
Vatican I (1869–1870)

As with all general councils, Vatican I did not meet in a vacuum, though many inside and outside Catholicism accused Rome of being out of touch. Despite stereotypes, the church had not taken on a siege mentality right after Trent; by the nineteenth century, though, the popes had made it clear they saw much of modernity threatening the church. In 1864, Pio Nono had issued a *Syllabus of Errors,* which condemned many ideas and movements that made the modern world modern: secularism, rationalism, nationalism, individualism, and the umbrella term "liberalism," which referred generically to a free hand in all political, social, and economic spheres. Adding to his sense of being attacked by the outside world, Pio Nono faced the Italian unification effort, which literally swarmed around the city of Rome and the papal states. More globally, the relatively recent invention of the telegraph increased the power of the press corps, whose members called for increased openness and information from the Vatican.

Within the church herself, two groups fought for predominance—although, to be fair, the variety of positions along the ideological spectrum disputes the idea of a monolithic "left" or "right." That said, it remains true that a small group of the most extreme "ultramontanists" backed total papal authority, sometimes almost rabidly, over the entire world. While absolutism was falling out of favor in many countries, these ultramontanists promoted a pope and papacy of utter supremacy that should command—and get—complete allegiance from the world's Catholics.

At the same time, "liberal" Catholics wanted a closer relationship between the church and modernity, one that embraced political, theological, and liturgical innovations, usually while keeping church and state separate. This latter group, which tended to be more progressive on many political and social subjects, fought the papalist ultramontanes. Liberal Catholics complained about what they considered the overcentralization of Catholic matters in Rome, describing the Vatican as a tower disconnected from the people around it.

With these multiple contexts, movements, and groups at work, Pio Nono called a general council that was more ecumenical than most of its predecessors—at least in the sense that more of the globe was represented this time. Almost 750 delegates attended, and Europeans made up about two-thirds of the assembly. Bishops also came in solid numbers from the "new worlds" that Europeans had encountered since Lateran V and Trent met in the sixteenth century. Almost fifty attended Vatican I from the United States, thrity from Latin America, and over one hundred from Africa and Asia, including fifteen from China and nearly twenty from Australia and the Pacific islands. While the Asian and African representatives were European (especially French) missionaries and not ethnically African or Asian, they could not fail to bring their pastoral experience of diverse cultures to Rome with them.

Like most general councils since the first millennium (except for Lyons II and the Florence stage of Basel-Ferrara-Florence-Rome), Vatican I was not really ecumenical, despite its more global reach. In advance of his council, Pio Nono informed Protestant denominations and Orthodox patriarchs (distinct from the sixty eastern-rite prelates who eventually attended) that Vatican I would convene. He suggested that his council was a fine opportunity for them to return to union with the Catholic Church. Not surprisingly, no one accepted this hedged papal "invitation."

Two logistical things were new at Vatican I. First, the international press and the telegraph, which did not exist for the prior nineteen general councils, would keep the public informed of events and, in some cases, agitate for particular sides in the debates. Second, for the first time in history a general council would meet in St. Peter's Basilica itself. Vatican I met not in the main body of the church, where Vatican II would sit a century later, but in a large side chapel. Microphones were not available at the time. At one point, the proceedings were interrupted for workmen to arrange temporary walls and improve the acoustics so the participants could hear what was going on.

Before the delegates focused on Vatican I's more controversial debates on papal infallibility, they worked on the document *Dei Filius*. This statement took a fairly balanced approach to the questions of modern scholarship and rationalism. It did not condemn reason per se, which some of the more ultramontanist and intransigent parties wanted in the spirit of the recent *Syllabus of Errors*. On the other hand, *Dei Filius* did speak against pure rationalism that operated outside the contexts of revelation and the supernatural. Rationalism divorced from faith, the statement asserted, could lead to materialism and atheism, two modern threats to religion. The document also said, however, that reason and faith are not in fact incompatible.

Papal Infallibility and Jurisdiction

But it is, of course, the debate and doctrine of papal infallibility and jurisdiction that have become synonymous with Vatican I. Pio Nono sought a strong assertion of papal infallibility and of the primacy of papal jurisdiction. He wanted to declare unambiguously the pope as the highest judge and decision maker in the church: No one could go over his head. The pope had the final say, he could judge all things and all persons, but he himself could be judged by no one. Specifically, Pio Nono's agenda included asserting that the pope ran the church in terms of her discipline and government, and that the pope could make infallible statements on faith and morals on his own authority. This idea meant that he did not require the approval of the church for his statements to be accepted as infallible and binding on the faithful. In practical terms, this approval would come when the church accepted or consented to his statements— and that might logically occur at a general council.

Though he had called Vatican I, Pio Nono did not like the idea of the faithful accepting or consenting to papal statements and actions. That principle made it sound as though the church as the entire body of Catholics or represented by a general council ulti- mately judged what was infallible or not. One may ask, of course, why the pope simply did not declare himself infallible based on the right itself; if he believed himself the church's highest judge, why call a council to agree if he did not think he needed its agreement?

Indeed, it seems very ironic for this debate to occur at a gen- eral council, for history relates how councils sometimes fought papal power. In the past, as we have seen, councils laid down creeds on their own authority without strong papal leadership, which is precisely what had happened at Nicaea I and Constan- tinople I in the fourth century. Constantinople III went so far as to condemn the late Pope Honorius I because he believed Jesus had just one will. In the second millennium, Constance deposed two popes and forced the resignation of a third. In dramatic fashion, Constance had struck a blow for conciliarism by doing what no pope could do on his own: resolve the Great Western Schism by engineering the election of a single, unifying papacy.

By the same token, history also shows popes exercising over- sight of conciliar documents, as when Leo I simply canceled canon 28 of Chalcedon in the fifth century because it raised the prestige of Constantinople nearly to that of Rome. The four Lateran coun- cils, especially Lateran IV, were definitely papal meetings. More recently, Pope Eugene IV, after a rough start at Basel in 1431 through 1433, took control and declared his meetings at Ferrara- Florence-Rome, not the rump assembly back at Basel, the authen- tic general council.

A hint at why Pio Nono chose a general council to pursue his papal aims and how he regarded this mixed conciliar history might come from *Dei Filius*, Vatican I's first document. In this statement, Pio Nono acknowledged some collegiality between pope and bishops at Vatican I by speaking of his work with the bishops in a general council—although he stressed the council met under him:

> But now it is our purpose to profess and declare from this chair of Peter before all eyes the saving teaching of Christ, and by the power given us by God, to reject and condemn the contrary errors. This we shall do with the bishops of the whole world as our co-assessors and fellow-judges, gathered here as they are in the holy spirit by our authority in this ecumenical council....

In the end, perhaps Pio Nono wanted to demonstrate that the world's bishops, and the faithful they represented and shepherded, were behind him on the issues of primacy of papal jurisdiction and papal infallibility. At a time when monarchy as a governmental structure was under assault, a monarch with support looked better, stronger, and more legitimate than a monarch without support. Moreover, the pope's ability to call, preside over, and control a general council served as a prime illustration of his authority in action.

When it came to treating the issues of papal jurisdiction and primacy, Vatican I's participants backed several positions, with nuances among them. The strictest of the ultramontanists, a relatively small group, believed every word from the pope's mouth was infallible, not just his rare and extraordinary statements on matters of faith and morals. The most ardent looked to Rome for a steady flow of such statements to establish the church as rock-solid in a world marked by change. As the bishop of Geneva put it, Jesus had three incarnations: in the virgin's womb, in the Eucharist, and in "the old man in the Vatican." Their extreme opponents, also a small group, did not want any statement about infallibility at all. On the whole, many delegates backed infallibility without agreeing with the most zealous ultramontanists that infallible statements should be frequent in the church's life.

One other position was held by a minority group of delegates, perhaps 20 percent of the total, known as "inopportunists." Many of these delegates did not necessarily challenge papal infallibility, though they were uncomfortable with the most extreme ultramontanists. Inopportunists did not believe the timing was right for an assertion of papal infallibility for several reasons. They saw no pressing reason to lay down a definition; the church, they argued, had long survived without one. They believed the statement might be potentially divisive both within Roman Catholicism and between Catholics and other Christians. Inopportunists feared a formal assertion of papal infallibility would solidify a barrier to Christian unity, especially with respect to Orthodox and Protestant Christians. Many also had questions about the theological and historical underpinnings of the doctrine; their concerns included Constantinople III's troubling condemnation of Pope Honorius I.

The discussions about papal infallibility and jurisdiction traveled across the spectrum of these opinions, but they consistently ran up against a determined Pio Nono. One anecdote speaks for many. In an important moment during the debate, a Dominican theologian and cardinal said that he believed in papal infallibility this way: What the pope taught was infallible, but the pope himself was not infallible. This theologian described the pope as a bishop with fellow bishops. The pope was head of the college of bishops, he acknowledged, but the pope should not act separately from the other bishops. Indeed, the pope must speak in consultation with the college of bishops, who also play a key role in—and are part of—church tradition. That night, Pio Nono called the cardinal to a face-to-face meeting and declared, "I am tradition. I am the church."

Over the course of three weeks, Vatican I's delegates debated the draft statement on papal infallibility and jurisdiction in a fairly open manner. Of those who spoke, thirty-nine supported the draft and twenty-six opposed it. Then the organizers thought it best to let participants speak just on the section dealing directly with the infallibility wording, since that was the main point of contention. Three more weeks passed, but the split remained about the same: thirty-five for the wording, twenty-two against. After nearly two months of drafting, debating, and revising—in public and in private—the council's delegates cast preliminary votes to see where things stood. This trial ballot revealed a council with a significant minority dissenting. A large number, 451, voted in favor of the statement, but 88 voted against it, and 62 voted to accept it with reservations.

As it turned out, the final statement voted upon, named *Pastor aeternus,* contained two major parts: primacy of jurisdiction and infallibility. Concerning jurisdiction, the statement repeated verbatim key parts of *Laetentur coeli* (1439), from the Florence stage of Basel-Ferrara-Florence-Rome, which described the pope's powers as full, from God, and extending to the church throughout the entire world. It also spoke against the conciliar idea, without naming it as such, that someone could appeal over the pope's head to a general council whose authority, by definition, would be higher than the papacy's. Again reaching back to history, this wording is reminiscent of Pius II's statement *Execrabilis,* which condemned conciliarism in 1460, after several decades of papal recovery from the schism, Constance, and Basel.

The debate on the second part, the section on infallibility, produced significant changes. First, the draft title referred to the "infallibility of the Roman pontiff," but this was switched to the "infallible teaching authority of the Roman pontiff." As that Dominican cardinal later dressed down by Pio Nono had said: The pope as a person was not infallible, but his ability to teach as pope was. Second, the pope's infallible teaching authority concerned matters of faith and morals, not the daily governing of the church or the pope's political role. The renowned phrase that invokes this authority is *ex cathedra:* when the pope teaches in his role as universal shepherd from the chair *(cathedra)* of St. Peter, whose successor he is and to whom Jesus had promised assistance. The pope had won an important point when the statement declared papal decrees "irreformable" in themselves and not from the consent of the church, which would probably occur at a general council. Ultramontanists and inopportunists could each claim a measure of victory in this wording.

More politicking and soul-searching followed the final formulation of the statement, with the result that about sixty bishops left Rome on the eve of the official ballot rather than vote against papal jurisdiction and infallibility with the pope himself sitting right there. On 18 July 1870, in a moment better than fiction, 533 voted for the statement and two against it during a ferocious lightning and thunder storm. When the final tally was announced, both men who opposed the statement approached Pio Nono. Luigi Riccio of southern Italy and the Irish-born American, Edward Fitzgerald of Little Rock, Arkansas, said to him, "Holy Father, now I believe." In the end, over the course of several months, those who had left Rome rather than vote against the statement made their assent known and some even received the red hat of a cardinal.

Vatican I was effectively over, though it was not officially adjourned. There was no time: The day after the vote the Franco-Prussian War broke out. Because France needed its military resources elsewhere, it could no longer protect Rome, as it had been doing; France pulled its troops out of the city a few weeks later. By mid-September 1870, the Italians moved in and took control of Rome and the papal states. Pio Nono had gotten his decree of papal infallibility in a general council, but the papacy found itself in a precarious position.

Looking back at Vatican I, we see that the debate surrounding the statement of papal infallibility overshadowed an understanding of the relationship among papal infallibility, the bishops' collegiality, and the church's teaching authority. Vatican I, in the section that dealt with primacy of jurisdiction, moved toward a partial explanation of this delicate balance. The relevant excerpts are very papal and centralized when it comes to obedience and the church's hierarchy. But it also clearly identifies the unity of the worldwide church as an important goal of the pope's centralized authority.

> ...[W]e teach and declare that, by divine ordinance, the Roman church possesses a preeminence of ordinary power over every other church....Both clergy and faithful, of whatever rite and dignity, both singly and collectively, are bound to submit to this power by the duty of hierarchical subordination and true obedience....In this way, by unity with the Roman pontiff in communion and in profession of the same faith, the church of Christ becomes one flock under one supreme shepherd.

Just a few lines further on, however, the pope recognizes a measure of each bishop's independence and own authority.

> This power of the supreme pontiff by no means detracts from that ordinary and immediate power of episcopal jurisdiction, by which bishops, who have succeeded to the place of the apostles by appointment of the holy spirit, tend and govern individually the particular flocks which have been assigned to them.

> Papal jurisdiction and episcopal collegiality can coexist easily or uneasily. Though its delegates discussed the issue in committee, and despite these sections, Vatican I did not completely and definitively settle the question of the relationship between the pope and the bishops. That piece of business was left for Vatican II to pursue.

Chapter 10
Brave New World, Brave New Council: Vatican II (1962–1965)

John XXIII was surprising in many ways. He was not a leading candidate for the papacy when Pius XII died in 1958; from what we can gather, he was elected as a compromise and caretaker pope. After all, at seventy-seven years old, what harm could this gentle man do? Surely no one expected him to leave a lasting mark on the church. As soon as he announced his name, however, eyebrows were raised. He chose "John XXIII," the name of the pope who ran away from Constance and was later deposed by that general council. This papal name had been dead since then, but Cardinal Angelo Roncalli was not a man bound by the past.

Less than three months after his election, this John XXIII in a surprise announcement related that as he had been praying the idea "ecumenical council" suddenly came into his head, although some accounts found indications he had been thinking about a council earlier, maybe even during the conclave that chose him. In any case, it was clearly his decision: He did not seek opinions about the advisability of Vatican II before calling it.

Preparations, Expectations, Innovations

In January 1959, the news traveled almost instantaneously in the twentieth-century world of television and radio, arousing curiosity and excitement—but anxiety among many members of the curia. The council's agenda developed over time in reaction to discrepancies that started emerging between the raised expectations of the world's diocesan bishops working in the field and Rome's curial bishops, who largely wanted as little disruption as possible. The curia hoped for a medieval, papal, Lateran-style general council where delegates mostly approved a papal agenda set in advance. The world's bishops, and apparently John XXIII himself, had something else in mind.

Very quickly, a leftover question from Vatican I surfaced: What was the relationship between the pope (and the curia) and bishops involved in pastoral service among the church's grass roots? Would Vatican II be a chance for local bishops to outmaneuver Rome's central headquarters, if by no other means than their larger number? How could the bishops exercise their role not only as local shepherds, but as part of a college of bishops sharing the concern of the pope, their fellow bishop, for the universal church? In pragmatic terms, where did the college of bishops fit into the church's teaching authority? Vatican I's theoretical *Dei Filius* and *Pastor aeternus* had not fully addressed these critical issues. Vatican II, it seemed, would provide a chance to clarify the answers and then apply them more practically. But the curial and diocesan bishops approached Vatican II with potentially conflicting clarifications and applications.

Part of the excitement, curiosity, and possible trouble for Vatican II lay in the fact that, as John XXIII said in announcing the meeting, it was to break with the past. Historians put the previous twenty general councils into four major types, with some councils qualifying for more than one category. First, general councils tried for unity, like Lyons II and the Florence segment of Basel-Ferrara-Florence-Rome. Second, general councils condemned heresies and set doctrines, which happened at the first several and at Trent. A third batch of councils met for very specific purposes: to meet specific challenges or address pressing issues. Constance resolved the schism; Trent responded to the Protestant reformations; Vatican I defined papal infallibility. Fourth, reform was the main concern of certain councils, though almost every one addressed reform in some way. The four Lateran councils and Trent may be classified as the most important of these reform councils.

John XXIII had from the first moment explicitly labeled Vatican II a "pastoral" council that was to be different from past general councils. He did not convene it to face a specific threat or to discuss a matter of faith and morals, but for the "enlightenment, edification, and joy of the entire Christian people"—obviously both clergy and lay, and not just Roman Catholics. He would invite people from all the Christian churches. By April and May of 1959, John XXIII was speaking of the council as a "new Pentecost" for a "new age."

John's innovative mandate led theologians, bishops, historians, and even the press to search for precedents. They studied the history of general councils and wrote books and articles for scholarly and popular audiences. Because of ecumenical expectations, many returned to the era of reformations to discover just what separated Catholics and Protestants. Some turned the pages of history even further back to reexamine the east-west division from the earliest church. Several generations of theologians and historians had already begun to return to the church's original sources, especially those concerned with the nature of the church and with liturgy. Only by looking back and renewing the church's traditions, they argued, could a church that was connected to her heritage, but also open to legitimate innovation, move forward.

These scholars found no real model for John XXIII's pastoral council. Indeed, it was a general council of many "firsts." There wasn't a dominant, complex heresy like Arianism to address, so the first millennium wasn't much help. The situations surrounding Trent or Vatican I were not very analogous to Vatican II. Lateran IV may have been the closest thing to a prototype. Though certainly not the massive reorientation Vatican II turned out to be, Lateran IV had been the culmination of a century's theological and reform developments—and that is precisely what Vatican II eventually became.

While the search for precedents proceeded, some became concerned that the initial excitement was fading or being blocked. In the years between John XXIII's announcement in January 1959 and his general council's first session in October 1962, it was not a foregone conclusion that Vatican II would be a council of unprecedented *aggiornamento*. Rome began to prepare for Vatican II by sending out an invitation to the world's bishops to give their opinions on certain items and to suggest others for discussion. Many of the bishops' reports challenged Roman and curial centralization. Episcopal opinions were largely practical and pastoral—and thus in agreement with John XXIII's ideas—but some diocesan bishops joined curialists who wanted a "good, old-fashioned" general council with doctrinal definitions or condemnations, like Trent and Vatican I.

The written opinions that diocesan bishops sent to Rome also indicated they wanted the church to adapt to modern times and diverse cultures, though they presented a great variety of ideas on how to accomplish this goal. Many bishops in the field favored liturgical renewal, too, especially an increase in the laity's active participation and the use of vernacular languages. Some expressed concern that Rome moved slowly, perhaps even stalled, and wanted to focus only on internal matters. They feared the curia was succeeding in narrowing John XXIII's broad and open vision.

All of these expectations, hopes, and curial actions cannot, of course, be separated from the late 1950s and early 1960s. A Cold War threatened the world with nuclear annihilation; in an astonishing coincidence, Vatican II opened on 11 October 1962, just a few days before U.S. president John F. Kennedy received the reports confirming Soviet missile sites ninety miles from America that led to the tense, two-week Cuban Missile Crisis. Around the world, challenges to authority were the norm; attempts at self-government were on the rise as Europe's current and former colonies, especially in Africa, struggled for independence. The world was marked by change, and John XXIII did not want the church left behind.

Moreover, technological advancements would affect the council. Press involvement was not entirely new because journalists had played some role during Vatican I, but certainly the scope of the media had evolved in two substantial ways. First, it was now a "mass" media with about a thousand reporters from all over the world looking not only at the big picture, but at their local bishops, what they were doing, and what the council's impact at home might be. Those reporters came not only from Catholic newspapers; the secular press showed increasing interest in what was happening, and their reporters were not always Catholic. This led to some misunderstandings from journalists who did not understand Catholic matters, but it also gave the coverage a more ecumenical perspective.

Second, the media was "mass" because it operated in more than print outlets. Now, for the first time in history, Catholics around the world could hear and see for themselves on television the events of a general council. Vatican II was the first general council to be surrounded by microphones, speakers, audiotaping, film recording, telephones, and electric lights. In yet another first for conciliar history, this general council met in the main body of St. Peter's Basilica.

All of these "firsts" helped make Vatican II a world news event that engaged Roman Catholics, non-Catholic Christians, Jews, Muslims, and people of all other faiths or none at all. The coverage showed viewers the largest general council ever. As many as twenty-five hundred bishops took part in Vatican II, with an average attendance of about twenty-two hundred. They truly represented the universal church, including relatively new Catholic communities in the developing world, which now had indigenous bishops. Europeans accounted for less than half of the assembly, Latin (Central and South) Americans for about a quarter, North Americans for a bit less than a quarter, and Africans and Asians for perhaps 10 percent each. Some bishops were able to attend from beyond the Iron Curtain. Nearly a hundred superiors of religious orders also participated. In addition, about five hundred theologians, historians, liturgists, and scholars of all ecclesiastical disciplines assisted at Vatican II, usually as experts *(periti)* advising individual bishops and committees.

Non-Catholic observers were an important addition to Vatican II. At the beginning of the council, thirty-one Orthodox, Anglican, and Protestant representatives were present. That total reached almost a hundred representatives from about thirty churches and denominations. They could not vote or address the council in its formal deliberations, but they attended the sessions and met once a week at a gathering of the Secretariat for Christian Unity, where they could speak. Many of these non-Roman Catholic Christians exercised great influence through informal conversations with diocesan bishops, curial officials, theologians, scholars, and journalists.

Opening Act

As Vatican II was just about to start, some pessimism filtered through Rome. The curia's documents and agenda had covered over the concerns of diocesan bishops; it looked like academic and theoretical subjects had replaced pastoral and practical concerns. Journalists groused because no one would talk to them. Most important, the world's bishops wondered about their tasks. Some feared Vatican II would turn out to be only a ceremonial meeting after all, with the diocesan bishops simply approving papal and curial decisions that had already been made. Moreover, not every bishop knew how to participate in a collaborative meeting—if Vatican II was going to truly be an international episcopal conference—because they had never experienced one.

Again, John XXIII surprised the church. He forcefully put himself behind a more open-ended vision of the council. In his opening address in October 1962, he said Vatican II must bring the church up to date and fight against the siege mentality that turned the church away from the world. More to the point, he warned against the "prophets of doom" who had a negative view of the current state of the world and the church's place in it. John XXIII made it clear which path he wanted the council to follow.

The curia, however, was not easily pushed aside by the aging pope. The council's first order of business consisted of voting for commissions of bishops to discuss particular topics. Curial officials had prepared lists of their favorite bishops, mostly from the members of the committees that had prepared for Vatican II. They hoped the council members would simply copy down the names of these bishops, whom the curia considered safe and sympathetic to its agenda. This plan might have worked: There was simply no way the council members would know 160 bishops (sixteen for each of the ten commissions) well enough to make a good decision as to which man was right for which task. The curia was banking on the council to defer to its choices, but something else entirely happened.

In a dramatic moment that matched John XXIII's bold words just a few days before, Cardinal Liénart, the bishop of Lille, suggested postponing the voting for several days so the bishops could get to know each other. This way, they could make more informed decisions and choose for themselves those candidates they considered appropriate for each commission. This proposal, which passed, helped diocesan bishops take control of the council away from the curia. Episcopal conferences from various countries quickly stepped in to introduce their members to one another, which led to more conciliar self-government. Now, bishops with pastoral experience from all over the globe would bring pragmatism, diversity, problems, solutions, and successful programs to the commissions.

The curia was not happy, but John XXIII was. Vatican II now rested in the hands of the world's shepherds, who from that point on did not hesitate to voice their opinions. The experience of drafting the document on missionary activity a few years later, for example, offers a prime illustration of episcopal independence at Vatican II. None other than Pope Paul VI spoke up for the draft, but the council's bishops overwhelmingly voted against it (and papal support) and sent the proposed text back to committee for an extensive overhaul.

Vatican II proceeded in this way during the four autumns of 1962 through 1965. John XXIII lived only for the first: He died in June 1963, and Paul VI was elected a few weeks later. The cardinals in conclave must have been preoccupied with a major question: What would the new pope do with Vatican II? Cardinals who did not like the turn the council had taken surely would have voted for someone who differed from John XXIII. Others obviously wanted the council to continue. Paul VI was a good choice because, though he had spent almost his entire career in the curia, he had also been a diocesan bishop and had a relatively progressive reputation. He quickly signaled his desire to see Vatican II proceed in its established direction, and he even went a little further by adding lay advisers. By 1965, about fifty laypeople had participated at Vatican II: Thirty men joined almost two dozen women, about half of them nuns.

Themes and Documents

Like Trent's three stages, which met over eighteen years, each autumn term of Vatican II had its own makeup, tone, process, conflicts, resolutions, and stories. Between the formal meetings each autumn, commissions met, theologians debated, proposals were repeatedly revised, journalists reported, and advocates agitated all over the world. This survey of the general councils cannot possibly convey the tenor of the particular segments and intermissions of Vatican II. It is perhaps best, for our purposes, to review the sixteen documents Vatican II produced, bearing in mind that summaries cannot capture the individual dramas played out as the council worked through each one.

This treatment of Vatican II's statements may seem disproportionate to that of the other general councils' documents. We will consider the most recent general council's documents at length for two major reasons. First, some numbers demonstrate an important comparison: Vatican II's documents are much longer than those of any other council. In the collection we have been using for this book, Vatican II's documents run to 315 pages—more than one-quarter of the total. Trent's statements, in second place, fall far behind with 139 pages, and Basel-Ferrara-Florence-Rome's come in at 136. Second, Vatican II's documents differ substantially from those of the previous twenty general councils. Most of the prior documents were very brief and directive: creeds, condemnations, definitions, rules. Vatican II's documents read more like mission statements that lay down general themes and perspectives. An entirely different tone permeates Vatican II's documents.

Historians like to call new approaches, like those found in Vatican II's long statements, "paradigm shifts": fresh ways of thinking that turn older ideas around. There are several paradigm shifts at work in Vatican II's words. For example, picking up on an early phrase of John XXIII, Vatican II often refers to a new era, a new stage in human life, and advances that sometimes proceed too quickly. History, society, and especially technology seem to be moving forward without a pause, making it hard for the world and the church to keep up. Change and innovation are the rule: Nothing seems to stand still any more, so people have to look at things anew.

The council said the church cannot afford to be left behind. If she wants to influence modern society, she must keep up and participate, while giving people a grounding and safe haven in the faith that does not change.

> ...[T]he church has the duty in every age of examining the signs of the times and interpreting them in the light of the gospel, so that it can offer in a manner appropriate to each generation replies to the continual human questioning on the meaning of this life and the life to come and on how they are related. There is a need, then, to be aware of, and to understand, the world in which we live. (*Gaudium et spes,* no. 4)

Along with the "signs of the times," the phrase most associated with one of Vatican II's paradigm shifts is *aggiornamento,* which usually is translated as "updating." This word, though, makes it sound as if once you update something, you don't have to do so again. A better translation is a more literal one: "to-day-ing." This word, while awkward, does remind us that *aggiornamento* is a constant process. Vatican II asked the church to institute an *aggiornamento* on two major levels: institutionally (as a church structure) and individually (as Christians). It is best, the council said, to approach the task of *aggiornamento* by respecting and drawing upon both the old and the new in tandem, not in opposition.

Another paradigm shift is the image of the church as a pilgrim. Vatican II repeatedly spoke of the church being on a spiritual and physical journey in this earthly life toward heaven in the next life. As such, she will make mistakes and stumble because she is both perfect and imperfect at the same time: perfect because established by Jesus, imperfect in that she is peopled by fallible human beings. The sixteen documents elaborated other shifts: a positive view of the modern world and culture; an increased role for the laity; the celebration of diversity; and outreach to other religions (Christians and non-Christians), to nonbelievers, and indeed to all of humanity. These themes transcend the sixteen documents Vatican II produced over its four autumns. We will take them in turn, although not in chronological order.

The Church and the World

Perhaps the most striking of Vatican II's documents is *Gaudium et spes,* concerning the church's relationship with the modern world. *Gaudium et spes* embraced the world's diverse cultures and recent developments. This document indicated that the church wanted to be the most open she had ever been to the world around her and that she was breaking away from a long-standing attitude of *contemptus mundi* (contempt for the world). The tone portrayed a church that is extremely aware of what is happening in the world and that would try to act differently from the disconnected, aloof, and out-of-touch institution she had sometimes been. But Vatican II did not just want détente with the world: It sought genuine engagement and dialogue.

The church's conversation with the world would consist of an attempt to read the signs of the times and respond to them. *Gaudium et spes* recognized the rich were getting richer and the poor were getting poorer. It recognized change, individualism, atheism, the threat of nuclear war, technological advancement, growth in a "scientific mentality" that was poised even to send human beings into space, urbanization and industrialization, and the demands for economic and gender equality. Rather than turn away from these massive shifts, *Gaudium et spes* directed the church to see them as opportunities for evangelization and holiness. Modernity could help the church and the church could help modernity; interplay between the church and the world would benefit both. The document also directed the church to protect the economic and political rights of everyone. At the same time, it focused on each person's inner spiritual renewal and on each person's obligation to help and serve others.

What Is the Church?

A second major document discussed the church's character and tasks, signaling a major thrust in its Latin title. *Lumen gentium* described Jesus as the light of the nations and wanted the church to spread that light throughout the world. The document explored the branch of theology called ecclesiology, which treats the church's nature and mission, especially her universal functions. *Lumen gentium* presented several images of the church operating simultaneously. She was both an institution and the mystical body of Christ, and was made up of clergy and laypeople, head and members, a hierarchy and a decentralized community of believers—all at the same time. The document also stated that the church as an institution and each of her members were on a pilgrimage, an idea that avoided some of the triumphalism occasionally evident at the councils of the first millennium and at Trent. In sharp contrast to the phrase *anathema sit,* which has colored perceptions of the church as intolerant (especially in her general councils), *Lumen gentium* cast a positive eye on all people who seek God by any path: Catholic, Christian, non-Christian.

An absolutely crucial section of *Lumen gentium* carefully addressed some of Vatican I's unfinished business: the relationship between the pope and the bishops, an affiliation that Paul VI himself wanted to see clarified. In its text and a special explanatory note that followed, *Lumen gentium* described papal primacy in words close to those of Vatican I's *Pastor aeternus.* But *Lumen gentium* also said the bishops are part of a college and enjoy apostolic succession, too.

The bishop is the "principle and foundation" of the unity of his local church (diocese), while the pope is the "principle and foundation" of the universal church's unity. When the world's bishops gather together in a college, they share in and assist the pope's universal concern, as when they gather in a general council.

Lumen gentium further delineated the integral connection between bishops and the pope. Bishops exercise the office of teaching and governing, but only in communion with their brother bishops and with the pope, who is simultaneously both a member of the college of bishops and its head. There is no equality between the head (the pope) and the bishops. Bishops cannot take collegial action independently of the pope: They must always be in communion with him. But while the pope gives bishops their assignments and has a certain oversight of them, they are not simply papal delegates: Bishops have their own authority and a certain independence. Notably, after repeating Vatican I on papal infallibility, *Lumen gentium* (no. 25) extended the principle to the college of bishops, too: "The infallibility promised to the church exists also in the body of bishops when, along with the successor of Peter, it exercises the supreme teaching office."

Laypeople and Education

Lumen gentium's words concerning laypeople as part of the church link this document with another, *Apostolicam actuositatem,* which discussed the laity more comprehensively. *Lumen gentium* (no. 33) taught that each lay man and woman had a Christian vocation: "The apostolate of the laity is a sharing in the church's mission of salvation, and everyone is commissioned to this apostolate by the Lord himself through baptism and confirmation." Pastors were to respect this fact and the laity's diverse roles, including their participation in appropriate ministries. Indeed, *Lumen gentium* said the laity should have the lead role in bringing Christianity to the workplace or other secular settings.

Apostolicam actuositatem explored these points by using the language of a lay vocation and by calling for lay service. In the modern world, the document taught, the lay apostolate had grown larger, more important, and more urgent. Women's participation in the church needed particularly to increase. A new department for the laity in the curia was established to pursue these lay goals and responsibilities, which *Apostolicam actuositatem* described in general terms.

Vatican II also taught that it was the layperson's job to bring Christianity outside the walls of the church in order to renew the world. A layperson's life and faith should combine within one focus: Jobs, family duties, social and service activities, and Christian principles should never be separated. *Apostolicam actuositatem* directed the laity to use their minds and nonreligious training and education to see Christianity at work in new questions, in modern situations, and in ground-breaking issues. It also called for more spiritual and doctrinal formation among the laity so their apostolates in the church and the world could expand and evolve.

In order to exercise their apostolate, the laity needed to learn more about the faith. In its statement on Christian education, *Gravissimum educationis,* Vatican II recognized the need for new methods of teaching and learning, but acknowledged that the bishops' conferences should work out and adapt such methods to local cultures. *Gravissimum educationis* taught that everyone has an inalienable right to education, but told parents that their role in educating their children about the faith was paramount. Vatican II spoke of the importance not only of Catholic schools, but of helping students in non-Catholic schools to learn the faith, too. Higher educational institutions should concern themselves with catechesis; everyone involved in education should always look out for talented teachers and young people who could be guided into the classroom.

Liturgy and Scripture

In addition to Catholic education and catechesis, one of the places where laypeople could especially increase their participation was in the liturgy. The document on liturgy, *Sacrosanctum concilium,* said it was the holy spirit who was increasing enthusiasm for liturgical renewal. Vatican II directed the church to adapt in the liturgy elements that could be changed, but to ensure that new things grew organically from old: Innovations, adaptations, and other reforms must not be cut off from the church's tradition. *Sacrosanctum concilium* several times advocated greater liturgical involvement and education of the faithful, who must "know what is going on." Everyone in attendance at a liturgical function should take a "full, conscious, and active part" in the celebrations.

Sacrosanctum concilium said the church should emphasize the communal nature of liturgies and that all should participate with fervor. It encouraged singing (accompanied by instruments other than just the organ) and frequent reception of the Eucharist. The document praised the diversity of devotions, left it up to the local bishop to decide on the advisability and benefit of introducing the vernacular language into liturgies, and called for simpler rites that returned to their origins. This document, more than any other, helped Vatican II's *aggiornamento* hit home.

Vatican II also treated scripture, another topic that touched people on a very basic level. The council's document on revelation, *Dei verbum*, echoes some of Trent's traditional language, as when it reminds Catholics of their reliance on both scripture and tradition.

> ...[S]acred tradition and scripture are bound together in a close and reciprocal relationship. They both flow from the same divine wellspring, merge together to some extent, and are on course towards the same end....[B]oth scripture and tradition are to be accepted and honored with like devotion and reverence. (*Dei verbum*, no. 9)

Along with scripture and tradition went the church's teaching authority, which guided Catholics' understanding and interpretation of scripture.

Scriptural understanding and interpretation had become more nuanced over the course of several centuries of study, particularly the hundred years prior to Vatican II. The council recognized this fact when it explained the process of scripture: eyewitnesses handed oral reports along to others who, over time, wrote down what they said. *Dei verbum* used the four Gospels as an example of this process. It also directed Catholics to utilize modern methods of scriptural study, especially by investigating the historical and literary contexts of biblical authors: their intent, genre, audience, and the sensibility of their ages. Vatican II wanted Catholics to explore scripture: the council encouraged vernacular translations and directed clergy especially to keep their own scriptural study current.

Bishops and Priests, Nuns and Brothers

Vatican II, like Trent, directed bishops to supervise many aspects of these renewals. The council encouraged the bishops' pastoral role in a separate document, *Christus dominus*. Picking up on some parts of *Lumen gentium,* this document described bishops as teachers primarily dealing with local matters, but who also must consider regional or worldwide issues when they meet with one another and the pope, as at a national synod or a general council. *Christus dominus* called for a reorganized curia with more international representation, a greater number of bishops with pastoral experience, and a willingness to listen to the laity's concerns. It asked bishops to direct their attention to catechists, their duties, and their training, which should include not only solid instruction in the faith, but also in psychology and pedagogy. Bishops should encourage the constant spiritual and educational growth of their priests and urge the laity to understand and exercise their unique apostolate.

A related document, *Presbyterorum ordinis,* provided a standard but lyrical treatment of priests' duties, spiritual health, ministry of service, and continuing education. It directed priests to be especially mindful of their role with respect to the laity: Priests should take the counsel of laypeople, respect their opinions and experience, and give them genuine responsibilities. *Presbyterorum ordinis* also defended and explained celibacy. Another connected document dealt with priestly formation. *Optatam totius* instructed local conferences of bishops to work toward a new program of priestly formation that emphasized regional situations and adaptation. This program must be devotional, intellectual, and pastoral. It should employ modern methods in psychology, sociology, and pedagogy in the discernment process and in the training and evaluation of seminarians.

In yet another associated document, Vatican II treated the renewal of religious orders. *Perfectae caritatis* encouraged orders of men and women to respond to modern needs and situations at the same time that they returned to, recaptured, and renewed their founders' original charisms and missions. One item that became a visible example of change had to do with habits of dress.

> Religious dress, the outward sign of consecration, should be neither flashy nor elaborate, but restrained and unaffected. It should meet the demands of hygiene, the style of contemporary fashion, and the practicalities of the apostolate. If the dress of religious, male or female, is unsuitable, it must be altered. (*Perfectae caritatis,* no. 17)

As with the liturgy, this aspect of Vatican II *aggiornamento* made the idea of renewal very clear to the eye.

Catholics, Christians, and Other Faith Traditions

These documents looked within Roman Catholicism, but the council also wanted to talk with others. Earlier general councils had contributed to the tensions between the church in east and west. During the first millennium, eastern churches objected when Pope Leo I canceled Chalcedon's canon 28 and when the west added the word *filioque* to the creed without a general council's approval. Other general councils, namely Lyons II and Florence in the Middle Ages, had tentatively mended the break, only to see unification fall apart almost immediately. Vatican II wanted to do better.

The open atmosphere and good spirit of Vatican II, along with the actions of Paul VI during and after the council, brought east and west closer together. The council's document *Orientalium ecclesiarum* wrote respectfully about eastern Catholic churches and noted that they, like Roman Catholics, recognized the primacy of Peter and therefore of the pope. In January 1964, Paul VI and Ecumenical Patriarch Athenagoras I met at the Church of the Holy Sepulchre in Jerusalem. In December 1965, the Orthodox east and the Roman Catholic west lifted their mutual excommunications of each other, dating from 1054, in a joint statement read simultaneously in Constantinople and Rome. In July 1967, Athenagoras I welcomed Paul VI to Constantinople; Paul VI returned the favor in Rome three months later.

Another of Vatican II's attempts at unity was the document *Unitatis redintegratio* on ecumenism, one of the council's principal concerns. Here Vatican II—teaching in an atmosphere and with an attitude entirely foreign to Trent's—acknowledged that there was plenty of blame to go around on all sides of the many-layered rifts between Protestants and Catholics since the sixteenth century. Vatican II reminded everyone that Protestants and Catholics share a common heritage in Christianity. *Unitatis redintegratio* sought dialogue in an atmosphere of reciprocal respect: Protestant and Catholic clergy and laity must treat each other fairly, learn about each other, pray together, and share social justice activities. The document also linked individual renewal, the church's *aggiornamento,* and ecumenism. The *metanoia* (change of heart) necessary for inner spiritual renewal should produce a generous spirit toward fellow Christians, which would in turn guide the first steps toward unity.

While some aspects of Vatican II focused on bridging the gaps within Christianity, others reached out to non-Christian faiths. With *Nostra aetate,* the church spoke about other faiths in a very different voice than she had used previously. *Nostra aetate* emphasized human commonality and the shared heritage of people who exercised any type of belief in the supernatural. Vatican II expressed Catholicism's respect for other faith systems, but it did not back away from its goal of sharing the good news of Jesus Christ. *Nostra aetate* spoke in favorable terms about Hinduism, Buddhism, and Islam, but some of its most striking departures from the approaches of earlier general councils dealt with the Jews.

Medieval general councils had restricted the offices and jobs Jews could hold, as well as the interactions between Jews and Christians. *Nostra aetate,* in a strong break with this aspect of conciliar history, said Jews and Catholics must seek "mutual knowledge and esteem," in particular by jointly studying scripture and theology as well as by engaging in "friendly dialogues." Significantly, *Nostra aetate* (no. 4) refused to label, burden, and persecute Jews with the charge that they killed Jesus, an indictment that had spoiled Jewish-Catholic relations for nearly two millennia:

> Although the Jewish authorities with their followers pressed for the death of Christ, still those things which were perpetuated during his passion cannot be ascribed indiscriminately to all the Jews living at the time nor to the Jews of today. Although the church is the new people of God, the Jews should not be represented as rejected by God or accursed....[The church] deplores feelings of hatred, persecutions, and demonstrations of anti-Semitism directed against the Jews at whatever time and by whomsoever.

Reaching Out

The council was charting a new course by reaching out to other faiths. At the same time, Vatican II concerned itself with living and spreading its own faith within three other contexts: the use of mass media, the activities of missions, and the exercise of religious freedom.

Inter mirifica, the statement on the mass media, viewed new technologies with optimism and excitement, not fear and loathing, as new instruments to spread the faith. It specifically called upon the laity to train in both new technologies and in Catholic dogma in order to get Catholicism's word out.

In *Ad gentes,* its document on missionary activities, the council tied missions with evangelization, a natural combination. *Ad gentes* stressed the unique challenges of spreading the faith in varied circumstances and recommended flexible, diverse approaches. Each new church should aim to be a self-supporting Catholic community: in communion with Rome, but also celebrating local customs in its liturgical rites. The missions should create an independent Catholic community as soon as possible with an indigenous clergy, permanent deacons, an active lay apostolate, and catechists who are well trained spiritually, doctrinally, and pedagogically.

Most of the activities, plans, and hopes outlined by these fifteen documents could only succeed if the church was free to pursue their programs. That need makes *Dignitatis humanae,* the statement on religious freedom, a keystone. Without religious freedom, which Vatican II described as a basic human and civil right, the church could not exercise the faith. People should be able to exercise their religious freedom as they should their basic rights to assemble, speak, and write freely. Recognizing that the church herself had not always been free of coercive actions in her history, Vatican II said religious freedom meant no individual or government could force people to gather religiously or to worship or believe a particular religion. People must be free to choose their faith or no faith at all. In more practical terms, *Dignitatis humanae* spoke against civil interference in internal church matters. Religious institutions and communities must be allowed to appoint, move, and train their own ministers; to deal with religious authorities in other countries; and to build, buy, use, and sell property. At bottom, Vatican II said there should be no discrimination based on a person's religious beliefs.

After Vatican II

These sixteen documents, as well as all the events and discussions that surrounded them, tell only the immediate story of Vatican II. The paradigm shifts and new ideas had to be carried out, and that is where, why, and how Vatican II has become a battlefield at the dawn of Christianity's third millennium. Of course, the rocky road of implementation had long before Vatican II become a familiar part of the history of the church's general councils.

Trent had tried to break with that history when Pope Pius IV set up a committee of cardinals to supervise Trent's program. But that committee did not necessarily help Trent's plan, for the cardinals tended to interpret Trent fairly narrowly and rigidly. After Vatican II, there was a commission on interpretation, although not in the powerful model of Trent's committee. One can argue, however, that even if Paul VI had recreated Pius IV's influential Trent committee, Vatican II had seen so much more episcopal and lay participation, such increased world attention, and so many more innovations and paradigm shifts that no one could have bottled the spirit of Vatican II with complete success, though some have tried. That is where Vatican II stands today, with some in the church saying she has moved too far too fast, while others believe she has not moved far enough and indeed has slowed down, if not reversed, her course. But the final legacy of Vatican II must be left to later generations to determine.

BIBLIOGRAPHY

Giuseppe Alberigo and Joseph Komonchak, eds. *History of Vatican II*. Maryknoll, N.Y.: Orbis Books, 1995–.

Cuthbert Butler. *The Vatican Council 1869–1870*. Westminster, Md.: Newman Press, 1962.

Avery Dulles. "Vatican II Reform: The Basic Principles." *Church* 1 (1985): 3–10.

Gerald M. Fagin, ed. *Vatican II: Open Questions and New Horizons*. Wilmington, Del.: Michael Glazier, 1984.

Rene Latourelle, ed. *Vatican II: Assessment and Perspectives, Twenty-Five Years After(1962–1987)*, 3 vols. New York/Mahwah, N.J.: Paulist Press, 1988–89.

Alberic Stacpoole, ed., *Vatican II Revisited by Those Who Were There*. Minneapolis: Winston Press, 1986.

Maureen Sullivan. *101 Questions and Answers on Vatican II*. New York/Mahwah, N.J.: Paulist Press, 2003.

Conclusions

This survey of the church's twenty-one general councils has tried to present each council in its own historical setting and as part of a cluster of councils meeting about the same time. But each meeting and group is part of a much larger story two millennia long. Before leaving this survey, we should pause and step away from these individual and group accounts to see the broader picture.

Despite the fact that the number "21" fits neatly into this twenty-first century of Christianity, as we have seen there has not been one general council each century. General councils are extraordinary occasions that do not meet according to any pre-set timetable—despite the schedule the Constance decree *Frequens* tried to establish. Although general councils have not been a regular feature on the church's calendar, they have been an important thread in church history.

While extremely important to church history, these twenty-one major meetings do not represent the only times the church met to respond to her many challenges. Local, regional or provincial, and even papal synods pre- and post-dated the general councils. So the general councils cannot be considered merely in isolation. Especially in the early and medieval period, smaller meetings functioned as pipelines for questions, answers, and ideas. Moreover, each of the twenty-one general councils had its own preparation period, the gathering itself, and then a period during which bishops, clergy, and laity in diverse locations tried to implement the council's goals, decisions, and plans. In addition, not every one of the twenty-one was immediately accepted as worthy to join the highest level of general councils. Even today, we might continue to wonder why the mediocre meetings of Constantinople IV, Vienne, and Lyons I still make the list.

At the same time, we must resist the temptation to place the more impressive general councils on a pedestal and take them out of their time frames. The twenty-one general councils met in particular settings and cannot be separated from their individual circumstances. The first sat just as Christianity was moving from persecution to toleration and then acceptance as the Roman Empire's only official religion. The next several centuries witnessed one general council following another relatively rapidly—eight in about 550 years—to progressively work out doctrinal statements and theological creeds. The medieval councils had a wider agenda and focused on quite a variety of topics: disciplinary matters, societal violence, reform, relations with Jews and Muslims, heresy, crusaders and pilgrims, power struggles with other monarchies, and legal independence and procedures.

Since the late Middle Ages, the world's contexts have especially shaped the church's general councils. The schism, conciliarism, and the Protestant movements heavily influenced the general councils in the era of reformations. After Constance, Basel-Ferrara-Florence-Rome, and Lateran V struggled with papal authority and conciliarism, Trent resettled the Catholic Church within an unprecedented situation in which Roman Catholicism no longer held a monopoly on Christianity. More recently, Vatican I and Vatican II took very different approaches to locating the church and her mission in the brave new world of democracy, individualism, secularism, and social and technological change. At the dawn of the third millennium, the church is still working out Vatican II's many paradigm shifts, some of which picked up where Trent and Vatican I left off—or had feared to tread.

While each general council faced specific challenges, several issues spanned many of them. Included among these is the relationship between the Latin west and the Greek east. Part of the tension was historical, dating to Constantine's decision to move his imperial capital from Rome to Constantinople. Language was also a barrier: At some points during the first few councils, easterners and westerners could barely speak with each other, let alone describe complex theological concepts such as the hypostatic union. Tensions grew when Leo I vetoed Chalcedon's canon 28, which put Constantinople second in line behind Rome and said both cities should hold equal privileges. When the west unilaterally added *filioque* to the creed of Nicaea I and Constantinople I, even after Chalcedon said no additions could be made outside a general council, the east took this as an example of Roman presumption.

East and west tussled throughout the centuries. Most general councils after the first millennium, in fact, cannot really be called "ecumenical" because, as we have seen, the east participated only slightly or not at all. In the Middle Ages, Lyons II and the Florence stage of Basel-Ferrara-Florence-Rome tried to address the central issues separating east and west directly: *filioque,* liturgical differences (leavened and unleavened bread), papal primacy and supremacy. Their resolutions and statements of unity, however, existed as words alone. These conciliar failures postponed unity. It was the open-ended atmosphere of another general council, Vatican II, that contributed to the efforts of Pope Paul VI and Ecumenical Patriarch Athenagoras I to bring east and west closer together during the 1960s.

A second issue cutting across general councils concerned liturgy and devotions. Many think of Vatican II as the first council to talk about liturgy. This popular misconception derives from the fact that most people-in-the-pews experienced Vatican II's impact through the vernacular mass, new instruments and music at liturgies, and the abandonment of some traditional devotions. These changes were usually presented as new and innovative—as breaks with the past. But general councils have addressed practical, grassroots piety almost from the first. Ephesus in the fifth century took on the question of Mary as *theotokos;* Nicaea II in the eighth century jumped into the fierce controversy over icons and relics of Mary, Jesus, and the saints. Trent returned to the issue, noting that its teaching on devotions was in continuity with Nicaea II. Trent backed veneration of the saints and the use of indulgences, relics, and icons. It stressed, however, that the faithful should exercise these devotions with moderation—without admitting that Luther's criticisms of alms collectors, indulgence counters, and peddlers of phony relics were justified.

A third major theme, often disturbing, that many general councils have shared concerns political involvement. Constantine, not the pope, called Nicaea I and went on to confirm, then publish its decrees. Irene dominated Nicaea II. Lyons I deposed Frederick II, who ironically had succeeded in opening pilgrim routes where the church had failed to do so. The railroading of the Templars at Vienne mars that council. Sigismund, and not one of the three popes, oversaw Constance. Only in the modern period were general councils able to slough off direct political influence, although Vatican I and II both operated within powerful secular contexts of change.

A mixed papal record comprises the fourth element common to many general councils. In the first millennium, Pope Vigilius's waffling is a troubling legacy of Constantinople II, as is Constantinople III's condemnation of the late pope Honorius. A major example of this element in the history of popes and general councils is the conciliar claim to ultimate church authority, which was at work especially in the fifteenth century. The general council at Constance, after all, achieved what three competing papacies (the Roman, Avignon, and Pisan/conciliar lines) could not: a unification of the papacy and an end to the Great Western Schism that had lasted nearly forty years.

But perhaps the most engaging theme running through the church's twenty-one general councils has been the attempt to balance the relationship between the pope and the general council and/or the college of bishops. Councils have often asked, implicitly or explicitly: "What is the relationship between the pope and the college of bishops—especially at a general council?" Conflicting versions of what happened at the "Council of Jerusalem" offer a double legacy from the very beginning. The Acts of the Apostles provides an account that seems to give James (but not Peter) the final say, while Paul's report in Galatians indicates a more collaborative example of decision making.

We have often seen these two models overlapping and even crossing swords in the history of the general councils. In the third and fourth centuries, regional synods, particularly in North Africa sometimes resisted Roman supervision. During the same period, the pope did not appear as a major player at a general council until the third one, at Ephesus. As popes increased their authority in the Middle Ages, they transformed general councils into occasions not so much for collaboration as for promulgation of Roman decisions made before bishops arrived at the Lateran meeting hall. But when the papacy wounded itself through the Avignon years, the schism, and curial worldliness, general councils stepped in to chastize the popes and, at Constance and parts of Basel, to take church power in their own hands.

The question continued in the modern period. At Vatican I, inopportunists supported papal infallibility and ultimate jurisdiction in theory, but many of them saw no point in forcing the issue by committing that authority to paper at their general council. Moreover, Pio Nono's meeting never answered a question logically related to its statements on papal authority: What was the correlation of papal to episcopal authority? For this reason, Vatican II in *Lumen gentium* (and the church in the revised Code of Canon Law) clarified that relationship, specifically as it would be operative at a general council.

In the end, the history of the twenty-one general councils is the history of the church's responses to challenges. At best, they provided opportunities for their members to gather together from diverse places to address common problems from a variety of perspectives and experiences. Vatican II best exemplifies this conciliar task, as it was the first truly global general council. At worst, general councils were defined by power politics, both within the church and between religious and civil authorities.

Not every general council settled the issues of its day definitively, though most met in honest efforts to solve problems. Implementing its solutions—the second act of each general council—was almost always another story. After a few, some Christians pushed conciliar definitions and programs so far that they ended up deviating from their orthodox creeds. This is what happened to Apollinaris after Nicaea I. In his attempt to fight the heretical Arian picture of Jesus as only a superman, Apollinaris emphasized Jesus' divinity so much he ended up teaching, incorrectly, that Jesus was fully divine but not fully human.

Other times, a general council's second act moved at a snail's pace. For example, Trent's most innovative aspect, the establishment of modern seminaries, proceeded very slowly. One study of Italy has shown that more than a century passed before Trent's order to set up seminaries produced substantial fruit. Sometimes, the speed and scope of the second act are themselves controversial. In the late twentieth and early twenty-first centuries, for instance, supporters and opponents (and those between these poles) accuse one another of pushing Vatican II's agenda too far or not far enough.

These examples remind us once again that a council's statements on paper take time to have an effect on flesh and blood, brick and mortar. For this reason, we should call the current period the "Vatican II church" and not the "post–Vatican II church," for the church is still living with the latest council. History's examples and patterns reveal the contemporary Catholic Church to be right where she belongs: working to put the most recent general council into practice, dealing with its legacy, responding to unforeseen reactions, and measuring herself against its thematic documents and directives. This may prove a bumpy road, but it is the same road general councils have taken in the past.

Index